Impact/Impasse

Impact/Impasse

Revaluing University Classroom Life

Laura E. Smithers, Heidi Fischer,
and Faith A. Watrous

Cover image: *Student (Costume Study for Goll's "Methusalem")* (recto), 1922. George Grosz (German, 1893–1959). Pen and brown-black ink (applied with the aid of drafting tools) and watercolor; sheet: 52.7 × 38 cm (20¾ × 14¹⁵/₁₆ in.). The Cleveland Museum of Art, Contemporary Collection of The Cleveland Museum of Art 1966.50a. © Estate of George Grosz/Licensed by VAGA at Artists Rights Society (ARS), NY. Courtesy of The Cleveland Museum of Art.

Published by State University of New York Press, Albany

For information, contact State University of New York Press, Albany, NY
www.sunypress.edu

Library of Congress Cataloging-in-Publication Data

Names: Smithers, Laura E., author. | Fischer, Heidi, author. | Watrous, Faith E., author.
Title: Impact/impasse : revaluing university classroom life / Laura E. Smithers, Heidi Fischer, and Faith A. Watrous.
Description: Albany : State University of New York Press, [2024] | Includes bibliographical references and index.
Identifiers: ISBN 9781438498188 (hardcover : alk. paper) | ISBN 9781438498201 (ebook)
Further information is available at the Library of Congress.

Hence if new modes of description come into being, new possibilities for action come into being in consequence.

—Ian Hacking, *Making Up People*

Contents

Preface

New Normals

We were a year into data collection for this book when the COVID-19 pandemic shut down and then sent colleges around the United States online, including our field site. This brings an unexpected structure to our book. Our initial vision of a tornado of short anecdotes from classroom life did not quite work, as classroom life across the span of our data collection became so radically different. Instead of a fever dream of classroom anecdotes from here to the index, we have structured these anecdotes into five chapters, or five artificially discrete fever dreams, bookended by an introduction and afterword.

The strange timeline involved also gives us another window into the work of impact in higher education: the role of conceptions of normal. The medical and social effects of the COVID-19 pandemic heightened calls for a new normal, instead of a return to the normal of fall 2019 and before, and in place of the constant upheaval of life at the beginning of the pandemic. We here collected classroom experiences in a high-impact practice from immediately before everything changed, when no one could have predicted what was to come, and immediately after, when everyone's predictions were built on scant historical precedent. Predictions came with the urgency that everything had changed, and this narrative made it hard to escape the implication that the before-times were stable, or normal, in the first place. We now finish this manuscript from within our new normal—or perhaps the old normal made new. We take on the discourse of the new normal throughout this book explicitly and implicitly. This book questions an aspect of normal unquestioned by the new critique: the normal of determining the value of a college education through measurements of college impact, measurements dependent upon and confounded by conceptions of student engagement and integrative learning. The normal of impact constructs our identities, our possibilities, and our everyday practices in higher education and has done so for generations. We ignore the stability of impact in our unstable time at our own peril. We prefer infinite new normals produced by continued revaluations of university classroom life. This book takes an insider look at the practices that become calculations of impact to access the impasses of ordinary, anecdotal student engagement in college. What follows is a slightly restrained fever dream in service of the revaluation of classroom life.

Acknowledgments

First and foremost, we owe a debt of gratitude to Senior Acquisitions Editor Rebecca Colesworthy, our incomparable guide and advocate throughout this process. Thank you for all you've done to help bring this book to the light of day.

We also want to thank all the beings in our lives who have cheered us on during the long and unpredictable journey of this project. Friends, family, colleagues, humans, pets—this book would not be in the world without you. Thank you, danke, meow, woof, et al. for your support.

And finally, we want to express our deep appreciation to all those who surfed the ordinary with us at our field site. For two years, you welcomed us into the life of learning communities at State U. We sat next to you in class, joined your Zooms, talked in hallways, and went on field trips together. You let us in on conversations in the back of buses, in the back of classrooms during class, after class, in Zoom chats, in sidebars during trainings, while walking together across campus, and in countless other interstitial spaces. Thank you one and all for your trust, openness, generosity, and kindness.

Prior versions of some sections of this book have appeared in the following:

Smithers, Laura, Heidi Fischer, & Lanah K. Stafford. "Ordinary Engagements: The Everyday Creation of a High-Impact Practice." *Journal of College Student Development* 62, no. 4 (2021): 405–21. https://doi.org/10.1353/csd.2021.0044

Smithers, Laura Elizabeth. "The Value of the Useless: Erin Manning, Impact, Higher Education Research, Progress." *Reconceptualizing Educational Research Methodology* 13, no. 3 (2022): 102–18. https://doi.org/10.7577/rerm.5146

Introduction

Everything is Anecdote

This book celebrates hunches and stubborn beliefs about student engagement and integrative learning in higher education and ultimately, but not centrally, the impact of college on students. Throughout this book, readers will encounter student engagement and integrative learning as hyperlocal ways of being, actions resistant to scale, and practices that elude the capture of surveys—in short, engagement and integrative learning as anecdote. In our data-driven times, anecdote is something to be remedied with the truth of metrics. In cultures of data, it is not that anecdotes are untrue per se but that only data captures truth that can be scaled, truth that can be the basis of decision making, and truth that carries institutional and policymaking value. In celebrating anecdotal, ordinary, banal, and otherwise unremarkable classroom experiences, this book relocates the value of higher education from data to the spaces in-between metric and anecdote, completion and hunches, GPA and stubborn beliefs, and importantly for a book about impact, student engagement and integrative learning as understood in relation to high-impact practices[1] and daily classroom practices.

The Problem: Our Values

This book addresses the disconnect in higher education between the values of quantification and affect, or our ways of being that resist quantification. In other words, it explores the spaces between models of high-impact practices and the squishiness of daily student life. For the last fifty years, the

1

value of higher education has been understood as a college's contribution to, or impact on, student outcomes variables. George Kuh's *High-Impact Educational Practices*[2] capitalized on this values system to name eight college practices that demonstrate the most quantifiable impact. The value of these programs at colleges across the country is now rendered through the label of high-impact practices. Simultaneously, liberal education, a concept that described the value of a college education before value was thinkable as measurable impact, has also been captured by algorithms and models. The language of the value of higher education has coalesced in the measurement of impact, forcing unquantifiable values either into its mold or casting them aside. In this time, college environments have privileged quantification and its abstraction of the human experience into the mobile data points that have come to define us.[3] In doing so, we have subordinated the values of college in excess of metrics to metrics.

This book presents a valuing of the student experience, whether we consider that experience to be student engagement or not, outside of components to be optimized for the production of student outcomes. Instead of turning to high-impact practices or other campus optimizations to determine what college practices have value, this book turns to the on-the-ground idiosyncrasies of daily practice as valuable in and of themselves. Instead of valuing everyday student experiences as moments to be added up to equal high-impact, this book values the everyday on its own terms as expressions of the world that makes *high-impact* possible. These anecdotes are singular practices that in the end generate impact without the algorithmic certainty of an impact calculation. Impact happens. The value of everyday impacts is not their statistical contribution to a high-impact practice; everyday student experiences are high-impact unto themselves. In revaluing impacts through these impasses, students, faculty, administrators, and practitioners also regain value in excess of their algorithmic contributions to the production of college impact.

College impact cannot continue to be the primary values system we as practitioners, administrators, policymakers, students, faculty, and the general public have for higher education. It is not that impact's associated values (e.g., retention and graduation) are valueless. It is also not the case that ordinary student experiences are always good. It is rather that we cannot continue to focus on the value of measurable college impact to the subordination and exclusion of all other values. Valuing college only insofar as its impact is measurable orients the work of campus actors toward its production and thus away from other possible values of the college student experience that escape the measurement of outcomes.[4] This subordination and exclusion also creates practitioner, administrator, and faculty value in terms of production of student outcomes, foreclosing student outcomes beyond measurement and linking staff performance judgments to these metrics.

The economic crisis sparked by the COVID-19 pandemic high-lighted once again the problems of the gig academy[5] and the valuation of quantifiable impact above most others: the most vulnerable campus actors for targeted cuts were not only disproportionately workers of color and contingent workers, but those considered to have a weak measurable impact on strategic priorities such as enrollment, retention, and graduation.[6] Discussion of a needed new normal in the wake of COVID-19 must not use the many faults of American higher education that preceded the pandemic to call for a new order of innovation led by data and just-in-time learning.[7]

Our alternate valuation of higher education does not simply point to more deserving members of a precariat or better methods for the precariat to access training needed to be slightly less but still very much precarious. It questions the very notion of a panic over enrollment numbers as the proper object of a higher education system oriented to the public good.[8] Most importantly, the alternative valuation we seek does not rest on any single desired new normal at all: it rests on endless new normals. This is endless experimentation driven by affirmation, or a desire to increase our collective positive potential in the world.[9] We urgently need new languages of value in higher education. Here, we follow the path of Michel de Certeau: that is, we bring "scientific practices and languages back toward their native land, everyday life." Across the anecdotes to come, we revalue the everyday life of learning communities.

A Problem: Impact

This book takes what has become the common sense of college practice, the turn to data-driven (and data-validated) practices such as high-impact practices, as its central problem. When the quantification of our practices drives their value, practices that can be quantified have value. These practices come to be equated with impact, an equation dominant in the study of higher education for the past half-century and that set the stage for the possibility of a category like high-impact practices to dominate.[10]

The idea of impact has captured the imagination of higher education in our time of late-stage capitalism. Impact is used to sell higher education as a site of action and something colleges make.[11] Impact sells a college as a site of value and something a college provides to its consumers.[12] Impact sells a college as serious and signals a college's commitment to data.[13] Impact sells a college as a location of positive affects and is the production of hopes and dreams, social mobility, a better life than previous generations, and the satisfaction of being a graduate.[14] In practice, impact is a value-added measurement—it is the value a college adds to a student above and beyond the growth they would have experienced over the same period without attending college.[15] In practice, this calculation forestalls the ability of colleges to make good on the promises of impact that they sell. Colleges that value impact structure their operations to provide impact to its consumers in a measurable form. Colleges provide credits, contact hours, registration within days of application, graduation within an on-time amount of terms, a particular number of high-impact practices, a sum of contacts, touches, integration, and learning or engagement units.

The problem with impact is that the promise and potential of college is more than the sum of these parts. Participation counts in high-impact practices may on average add up to higher rates of on-time graduation,[16] but what does that credential reflect?[17] Graduates may improve on measures of social mobility,[18] but what does social mobility mean in the Second Gilded Age in America, where social, income, and wealth inequality are at unprecedented levels? The impact of college is somehow both present and never present enough. Its manufacture is not only necessary; also necessary is its predictive manufacture. Colleges must predict spaces of non- or negative impact before they happen and preempt their emergence, sliding even out of the calculations of impact to logics of anticipation and affects of fear.[19] Impact creates its own unsolvable problem, and meanwhile, larger societal values of democracy and equality are in peril. Impact is an insufficient measure for our times—but more than this, impact is an insufficient value for our times.

High-impact practices, and the conception of student engagement on which they depend, have turned student affairs practitioners in particular into interchangeable widgets in the age of the completion agenda.[20] Given the imperative of the completion agenda is the production of student success as graduation, the value of student affairs practitioners and other college actors is in their contribution to this metric. Academic advisors are becoming success coaches;[21] orientation and first-year programs directors are becoming navigators and onboarding specialists,[22] ad nauseam. Metricized value leaves practitioners, administrators, and faculty increasingly vulnerable to the rise of learning and predictive analytics in higher education. If staff and faculty positions are widgetized, they can be digitized. Under this logic, all campus actors are one optimization away from being replaced by dashboards, automated text messages, generative artificial intelligence chatbots, and the like. Without alternative conceptions of value, the worth of campus actors is their contribution to metrics, nothing more and nothing less. It is time to revalue campus life.

Our Way Forward (Or Around and Around): Impasse

An everyday anecdotal impact focuses on all the ragged edges of college life within a high-impact practice. Anecdotes intervene against the abstraction of data—or the widget—to express its singular shapes and practices. Everyday impacts are transformative but not quite individualized, as the everyday conditions our possible individualized outcomes. The everyday creates the set of possibilities for the beings we might one day become. A conception of high-impact practices through anecdotes, the *stuff* of an impasse,[23] carries this significance: anecdotes are narrations of campus practices that feed and exceed the metrics that come to represent their value.

In what follows, we explore the value of classroom communities in terms of impasses rather than impact. To value the ordinary impacts that constitute a high-impact practice requires a commitment to the anecdotal that permeates every subsequent representation of such practices. Our focus here is on learning communities,[24] a high-impact practice whose value, once justified in other terms, has become enmeshed within the concept of high-impact practices.[25] Learning communities are spaces of possibility: if they indeed produce engagement and integrative learning that is high-impact, they do so in the daily grind of their production. Our work here is to step back from taken-for-granted structuring devices like *student engagement, integrative learning,* or *high-impact practice* to explore the everyday flows of affect that later form the student survey responses that adjudicate these structures—or not.[26] For Kathleen Stewart, the significance of the ordinary "lies in the intensities they build and in what thoughts and feelings they make possible. The question they beg is not what they might mean in an order of representations, or whether they are good or bad in an overarching scheme of things, but where they might go and what potential modes of knowing, relating, and attending to things are already somehow present in them in a state of potentiality and resonance."[27] To approach the ordinary is to experiment with all the fragments that give learning communities their impact as a *high-impact practice.* The ordinary are the anecdotes embedded in (and escape the gaze of) data-driven high-impact practice adjudicators.[28] Structures like *high-impact practices, student engagement,* and *integrative learning* drive change through higher education with the promise of their scalability[29] and portability.[30] The ordinary presents an alternative to scale. Impact happens in a million everyday moments that tend to escape our attention, anecdotes that we otherwise attempt to make linear and scale. Christina Sharpe discusses these as the atmosphere that conditions experience, the atmosphere of anti-Blackness specifically.[31] This atmosphere is present here within our orientation to the atmosphere of the student experience; it too creates the weather of this book. The ordinary privileges these impasses: the times in which linearity crumbles, and progress is relegated to a holding pattern.[32]

For Lauren Berlant, the impasse "is a space of time lived without a narrative genre";[33] impasses within learning communities are spaces of time lived without *student engagement, integrative learning,* or *high-impact practices* as structuring devices. More specifically, the impasse is "a stretch of time in which one moves around with a sense that the world is at once intensely present and enigmatic, such that the activity of living demands both a wandering absorptive awareness and a hypervigilance that collects material that might help to clarify things, maintain one's sea legs, and coordinate the standard melodramatic crises with those processes that have not yet found their genre of event."[34] In an impasse, we move without going anywhere, we sense but cannot make sense, and our presence in the present is such that connections to past and future constructs become opaque. The impasse denies valuation of college environments through impact, as the calculation of impact requires linear forward progress in which we make sense of the present through connecting it to past inputs and its effects on future outputs. The impasse orients us to a now where such concepts fade and, in so doing, creates space for new descriptions and modes of being to emerge. To engage in experimentation with the anecdotes of learning communities is to create their value in excess of their contributions to the measurement of high-impact practices.

Value and Revaluing:
Everything is Anecdote

The site of this book is a learning communities program at a public university in the mid-Atlantic United States. Learning communities are our site of interest for several reasons, the first of which is that they are labeled a high-impact practice, and their value on campuses is now commonly understood in relation to those terms.[35] This has not always been the case. Again, learning communities were once valued for something other than their contribution to metrics of engagement, retention, and graduation,[36] and learning communities can again be valued for something more. We can no longer only come to the value of higher education through quantification. Ordinary affects,[37] the ways in which we are moved as campus actors that escape the capture of quantification, are this book's mechanism for revaluing learning community classroom life. We sidestep the allure of causality as the story to be told about the value of college or, specifically here, learning communities.[38] We turn our attention to ordinary stories about college. We orient to the anecdotes that are in fact our contact with reality, our unobstructed experiences with learning and classrooms and growth and development and change. For Joel Fineman, the anecdote, "as the narration of the singular event, is the literary form or genre that uniquely refers to the real."[39] Anecdotes tell real stories. They are neither purely representational nor abstractions. Quantification abstracts ordinary life to create data-driven truth. In expressing the ordinary through anecdote, we live on the surface of truth-in-the-making.

Foci on high-impact practices (and both student engagement and integrative learning) rewrite co/curricular learning environments across higher education. This has been the case for over a decade and shows no sign of slowing, particularly in a renewed age of economic crisis and the ongoing analytics revolution in higher education.[40] An everyday intervention in this space, or a way of conceiving of good practices without reference to abstracted best practices, will be of interest to practitioners looking for alternative frameworks for understanding their role, as well as students and faculty in higher education and student affairs graduate preparation programs looking for a new frontier for high-impact practices. Theoretical work in education ignores this mundane space at its own peril. Higher education administrators who are pressed to develop interventions that have a quantitative impact on graduation rates, and by extension pressed into purchasing the time of consultants and the products of vendors to produce these, will welcome an alternative way of thinking through impact and their responsibilities to students.

The Structure of This Book

This book will take readers inside the impasses of nonresidential learning community classrooms at a public four-year university in the mid-Atlantic United States. Hereafter, this institution is referred to as State U. These impasses comprise the very anecdotes that come to be known as impact. These ordinary moments are woven together with an eye to move, or affect.[41] If ethnography means a manuscript generated through long-term participant observation with an eye to thick description, then this is an ethnography.[42] In practice, what follows is a thoughtfully messy admixture of ethnography, narrative inquiry, postqualitative inquiry, critical theory, low theory, cultural studies, and word on the street that finds its expression in anecdote.

Data comes primarily from our observations of learning communities in the Fall 2019 and Fall 2020 semesters; learning communities at State U. are almost always single-semester experiences. In Fall 2019, we observed two courses in each of four nonresidential learning communities for the duration of the semester. Of the two three-credit courses and a one-credit course that comprised each of these communities, the three-credit and the one-credit courses were observed in each community. In Fall 2020, we observed four of the five learning communities offered that term, each sharing the observed three-credit course and having their own one-credit course. The three-credit course this year was the same course and same instructor observed in two different communities in the prior year. In addition, we observed several peer mentor meetings, class field trips, class-related on-campus excursions, and learning community faculty trainings. We also conducted formal and informal interviews with learning community students, faculty, and staff and one focus group with students.

From these experiences, we re/present the mundane, ordinary moments that cohere as student engagement, the glue that produces impact,[43] as well as integrative learning, a value of learning communities that comes prior to their naming as a high-impact practices and also operationalized within the structuring device of high-impact practice.[44] These ordinary moments are expressed as a series of anecdotes from the learning communities program. Following Stewart, each anecdote "is a tangent that performs the sensation that something is happening—something that needs attending to."[45] These sensations in excess of representation central to this study are affects.[46] In attending to affect, we renarrate engagement to the banal in order to attend to the possibilities of the everyday. These anecdotes as a collection cannot be read as totaling to student engagement, integrative learning, or a high-impact practice. And still, they do. The ordinary can coalesce "into what we think of as stories and selves. But they can also remain, or become again, dispersed, floating, recombining—regardless of what whole or what relay of rushing signs they might find themselves in for a while."[47] We present these anecdotes as an engagement with the everyday. The structure of these follows our call for endless new normals. We offer these anecdotes lined up end by end, not necessarily in chronological order, in the spirit of affirmation and the impasse.[48] This is an and . . . and . . . and . . . approach to the value of college environments.[49] We present an alternative valuing of the higher education experience than those of structures that scale and multiply to optimize higher education.

Our commitment to re/present affective, ordinary impact within and integration of learning communities manifests in several additional ways. First, where we can, we do not name people or groups, and we use pseudonyms otherwise. This applies to participant names, learning community titles, and course titles. This obscures an important politics of individualized location; however, this also opens an important politics of collective and social location.[50] We also refer to ourselves as *she*, in following with Stewart's example, to differentiate ourselves in our identities as researchers from subjects that arise "as a daydream of simple presence."[51] As researchers, we might pursue cause and effect, meaning, structuring devices, or impact; as *she*, we attune to the possibilities of what each anecdote might bring.[52] Just as we are against the imperatives of cultures of evidence to abstract the value of college environments through metrics, we are against extracting ourselves from the narrative that follows. This book is not about us, but it is also not without us. Our presence as *she* in what follows is as imperfectly represented in these pages as everything else. As our individual identities blur through these re/presentational moves, the possibility within the ordinary becomes palpable. Palpable here directly refers to the state between imperceptibility and categorization; it is a felt sense that has not yet found its *narrative genre* or structuring device.[53] This is the work of anecdotes: not to point to what learning communities, student engagement, integrative learning, or high-impact practices might mean but rather to attend to the worldings they make possible; worldings outside of our wildest imaginations for ourselves, our students, and our institutions; and worldings we can feel present in every moment if we can attend to them.

This book contains five chapters and an afterword. Chapters 1, 2, and 4 are anecdotes from learning communities in Fall 2019 as well as preparations from Spring and Summer 2020 for learning communities the next fall. Chapters 3 and 5 also contain anecdotes from the in-between time of Spring and Summer 2020 in addition to anecdotes from learning communities in Fall 2020. There are five types of anecdotes in each chapter. Student anecdotes and faculty, administrator, and student staff anecdotes do as they say: each type focuses on the activities of the named actors. The third type of anecdote is pedagogy. These anecdotes blur the lines between types of actors by primarily orienting to the social field at hand. The fourth type of anecdote is high-impact practice components. These components are framed by one of the eight components of a high-impact practice.[54] The fifth type of anecdote is explicitly theoretical. These surface both the practical comings-together of the book as well as the theoretical interventions of the other four types. We do not name anecdotes by type in the text.

We urge readers to get lost in the organization. There is no master narrative we are crafting through the ordering of anecdotes. We also urge readers to read these anecdotes as something other than a simple reprinting of our field notes. Each anecdote comes from fieldwork and is a *literary*[55] expression of the world of the learning community under study as mediated by us. Field notes, be they observation notes, interview transcripts, or otherwise, generally attempt to re/present the world presented to the researcher recording them. Anecdotes are not representational projects; in their commitment to the literary, they are affective interventions. Anecdotes transmit, imperfectly, the affect of the world they track. Everything is anecdote. Structuring devices help us make order of these. Where impact asks us to begin from structuring devices to engineer pasts and futures that comport,[56] liberal education demands attention primarily to anecdotes and subordinately to the experimentations with structuring devices they incite.

To the Impasse

In revaluing the methodologies we use to research educational environments, we revalue the environments themselves. This book is both a demonstration of research design and a meditation on the value of higher education. Our conceit is that each needs the other. To revalue higher education through research, we must adapt our research practices such that the expressions of alternative values become possible. This is the main register of this text. Another world is not only possible, but it also already exists. If it is valuable to highlight this re/valued higher education in research, our research practices must be capacious enough to attune to it.

It follows that if this revalued higher education is worth pursuing, then the reach of work like this must extend beyond traditional readers of research methodology texts. Readers who come to this text primarily through interest in the practicalities of revaluing higher education in excess of measurements of impact should feel free to dive deep into the anecdotes. Bounce around in and out of page order with abandon. Microdose the few interspersed theoretical anecdotes as you desire. Allow what you read here to alter your orientation to what matters in your daily practice. Come back to read this on a methodological register when it speaks to you; it will be here waiting.

We were not interested in writing a book about theoretical alternatives to impact that shied away from practice. We were also not interested in writing a book about practical alternatives to impact that shied away from theory. Most of what follows are practical anecdotes from classroom life. These perform the theory of the book. Some of what follows are theoretical readings of practice. Our task was to attend to everything that moved us, in all directions moved. These affects come from the stories, and they also come in between the lines; in the connections made; in the lingering questions unresolved on the page; and in the feelings of urgency, crisis, monotony, boredom, and everything in between. Our need to revalue higher education is urgent. What follows is a deep dive into the irreducibly qualitative[57] value of higher education.

Chapter One

Impact (2019–20)

Education Before the Call to Order

I.

In the two minutes before class starts, there is peer-to-peer advising on second-language degree requirements. There are also some other, quieter, conversations happening at other tables.

II.

In the two minutes before class starts, the instructor has already placed people in groups, each group seated together. She passes an attendance list around the room.

III.

Class starts in ten minutes. About thirty students are already here. No less than ten students attempt to swipe or scan into class as they arrive. This is an early class, and there is a strong group energy around bringing Chick-fil-A into class to consume for breakfast. She gets a closer look at what exactly the object of this energy is. Perhaps these are chicken biscuits being consumed? There are at least two chicken biscuits being consumed in her line of vision to the podium. There are at least five Chick-fil-A bags in class so far and counting.

IV.

Class has begun, but has it really begun in this room before the student who never brings a backpack arrives? He isn't too late today: it's only two minutes into class. Last time the only items he brought to class were a pack of Pop Tarts and water in a single-use bottle. Today, an upgrade: he has another water bottle, as well as a purple composition book and a mechanical pencil along with it.

V.

Class begins right on time with a roll call. A call to order of the most ordinary form.[1]

VI.

"It's 9:31, I think we can start."[2] Her watch says 9:29. The instructor was counting students in the room when she arrived at 9:25.

VII.

A question rings out on the bus en route to a local workplace relevant to the learning community theme: "Does anyone want to pre-order JoJo Siwa tickets with me?" His question is met not so much with disdain or with joy but with a shrug from his friends. Their conversation continues.

VIII.

Class begins one minute early, with the instructor welcoming those present. Three students enter at the posted class time, both on time and late.

IX.

She talked with the peer mentor in the five minutes before class begins. They discussed traffic on the busy road at the border of campus, where to park for free in the vicinity of campus, and optimal environments for homework. They agree on this last point: it's not at home. The peer mentor gets notifications from Netflix on her Apple Watch.

X.

For the first few weeks, her notes start mostly with the call to order. She too is disciplined, too formatted.

XI.

She arrives to class two minutes early. The students who walk in behind her go directly to the attendance box by the door and swipe their student identification cards. The instructor passes around attendance sheets for students to write down their names: an analog orientation to surveilling. Students continue to swipe in: a digital orientation to being surveilled.

XII.

The instructor once again adjusts the lights from the back of the room before class begins. Today, he lowered them to make the room darker in the front. This room feels like a Las Vegas casino; from within, there is no indication whether it's day or night outside. A disorientation to circadian rhythms, an orientation perhaps to lecture format.[3]

Engagement

What does Engagement look like? We perused the academic literature on the topic and found a variety of definitions, from time spent on task to the various data-driven student success measures and critical perspectives.[4] But after hours of reading and taking copious notes, one thing remains unclear: What does Engagement look like in real life? In the classrooms, in the hallways after class, across campus, and in the dorms? Can you touch it? Smell it? Taste it?

One day, the class meets in the library, and students are asked to participate in a scavenger hunt to familiarize them with the building and its resources. Students text pictures once they find each item, and these texts immediately show on the screen in the meeting room where she sits and observes. A group that hasn't yet left huddles together, shoulders hunched, speaking in hushed tones. Images flash on the screen of students posing with their items. Selfies. Big smiles as they complete their tasks. Both might be indications that the students are Engaged. Are they?

Another day, a student is sitting at his single desk in class. On his desktop lies a lone pen. No notebook, no laptop. Just his pen. He writes down nothing. Yet he has an answer for every open-ended question the instructor tosses to the class. So much so, that the instructor scans the room for other willing students before acknowledging lone pen student yet again. Just by looking at him in a snapshot, she would not say he was Engaged. But is he?

In a third class, a guest speaker drones on. Students are leaned back in their chairs; some have their arms crossed. She sees a few cellphones. Suddenly, the lecture gets spicy. Students are outraged, growling their disbelief in harsh tones. They looked disEngaged. But were they?

Connections

This instructor strives to make her course content relevant to the students' majors. She teaches at a university that requires students to take a variety of liberal arts courses to earn their bachelor's degrees. She believes in tying the course content to the major path where possible. The learning community in which she teaches has students from one single field of study. This helps. The instructor wishes that students were further along in their degree so they could benefit even more from the interdisciplinary nature of learning communities. But they are not. They are first-semester students at State U.

Progress Report

"They don't trust you at first," one person says, sharing their experience from last year.

The peer mentors have gathered with learning community staff for their monthly check-in. Seven peer mentors sit around a boardroom-style table in a small conference room, along with three administrators. The atmosphere is generally pleasant, although the students appear to be somewhat subdued.

She learns that the peer mentors are asked to organize two events for their learning community students this term: one academic, one social. Their goals, the mentors are told, are to provide a sense of community, to help the students identify personal goals, and to encourage campus involvement.

One of the administrators asks, "Is there anyone who doesn't have any ideas about what to do?" She is met with silence. The peer mentors look at each other and say nothing in response. For most of them, it's the second year of serving in their mentorship roles, so maybe they are comfortable with what is asked of them.

The meeting shifts to the solicitation of feedback about what is and isn't going well so far this term. The peer mentors' list of successes in connecting with their students is short. "We did a dream draw," one of them shares, "and they got to draw what they wanted to do after graduation. A lot of them wanted to go to professional school. And I felt like they really understood what the major entailed." Another mentor reviewed all of the syllabi for her learning community and plans to send reminders for assignments due. This goes above and beyond the expectations set for peer mentors by staff. She is hopeful this will result in her students connecting with her.

The remaining peer mentors' stories are fairly grim in comparison. "Only twelve students joined my GroupMe. They don't talk to me much," shares one disappointed mentor. Another chimes in with suggestions for how to be persistent, such as mass emails, reminders, or GroupMe text reminders. "My first-year students are veeery social," adds the student sitting between the two. This quip is met with chuckles around the table.

"My problem is to connect with them a bit more. They're kinda quiet." The three administrators nod in response to this remark but don't say anything in return, simply allowing the peer mentors to voice their challenges. The next mentor's contribution is more confident: "No issues so far. But could we provide a workshop for how to deal with a bad professor? Almost everyone in my learning community joined the GroupMe, and they talk about classes on there. They all came together against that . . . teacher." One administrator responds in the affirmative. Yes. She is happy to provide such a workshop.

Will this intervention incite change? Maybe the next update meeting will tell.

First Day, Take One

It is day one of college for most of these students and day one in their first learning community class. Students sit at high-school-type individual desks. The desks are uncomfortable, but that part is likely a familiar feeling for the students. Quiet. It is so quiet. Is it an awkward silence? She is almost certain it is. You can hear the proverbial pin drop. Anxiety and nervousness shimmer in the room: it flickers in the corners, on the surface, in the spaces between the backpacks and purses on the floor. The instructor is busy arranging items on the desk in the front of the room, taking an occasional sip of water from a reusable water bottle. The clank of the bottle rattles the silence, pinging around the room before settling back down into silence.

Class starts on time. The instructor explains that her class will coordinate with the other two learning community classes in the sense that the assignments will be related to the students' field of study. There are no visible or audible reactions from the students. Are they listening? Do they hear? Do they comprehend what a learning community is? That's the only reference to the concept of the learning community in today's class. The instructor begins the syllabus review, encouraging students to ask questions if something is unclear. They do not.

The instructor reviews her policies on late assignments and late arrivals to class. She bursts into a coughing fit, hacking into her hand while trying to regain control of her body. Her cellphone rings; she silences it. None of this seems to generate any reaction from the students. They continue to sit in silence. It's as if all the air has been sucked out of the vacuous classroom, and they couldn't be heard if they tried. If this is any indication, it will be a long semester.

The instructor wants to show students how to access their free text-book in Blackboard. She encourages them to take out an electronic device to access the system, and there is a general shuffle from book bags as they do so. Blackboard is displayed on the screen in front of the classroom as the instructor searches for the location of the text. "Anyone see the link?" she asks. No response from the students. They all have laptops on their desks or cellphones in their hands and are actively searching for the textbook.

When the instructor finds the link, she demonstrates where to click to access the class. Unfortunately, multiple students have trouble logging in. "Should we make an account?" The first student comment rings out. It's as if a watermelon has been smashed onto the ground and bits of flesh fly everywhere. The instructor attempts to help students log on. There is general chatter while students try to help each other access the book. Class concludes with the following instruction: "Plan a two-minute introduction of yourself for class Wednesday!"

Smells Like Team Spirit

All learning communities are not created equal at State U. There are those communities where students both live and learn together. There are those that combine developmental courses with credit-bearing courses. There are those that take place beyond the students' first semester in college. All of these community types are beyond the scope of our study. The communities we observe are taught primarily to first-year students, contain three linked courses, and are encouraged to have at least one integrated assignment.

Increased student Engagement is one of the institutional leadership's goals for learning communities at the university. The learning community cohort model can create a sense of team spirit among students.[5] Students create interpersonal connections by creating study groups and having a network of friends with which to share meals, attend social or athletic events, or navigate first-semester challenges. Across universities, learning community students form supportive groups.[6]

In the academic literature, this type of Engagement is often self-reported by the students.[7] Universities administer surveys at the end of the first semester or during the second semester of a student's senior year. They attempt to capture Engagement with numeric measures: a rating on a Likert scale.[8] But what does student Engagement do in all the anecdotes left untouched by this self-reported score?

Team spirit rating = 3.475.

We believe there may be more to it than that.

That Which Comes Before Denouement

"Cellphones away" comes the command from the instructor at the back of the classroom. This is a serious day it would seem. There are two men at the front of the room. They appear to be friendly. The more seasoned looking of the two is smiling. He has a kind face and seems happy to be there. The younger man is seated at the instructor's desk, ready to advance the slides.

The gray-haired, kind-faced man addresses the class, introducing himself and preparing the students for what's to come. "If at any point you're uncomfortable," he says to them, "you can get up and leave." Ominous words.

Excitement simmers on low near the floor of the room. No sparks, just the barest shimmer of electricity.

"You're going to have uncomfortable conversations," the other guest speaker chimes in. More ominous words. To break the apparent tension, the first man makes a joke about not wanting to call the folks he works with "sex clients" on the witness stand. It's borderline . . . something. There are a few light chuckles in response before the room falls silent again.

The guest speaker starts out by providing information about his work. Supervision levels are ranked high, elevated, medium, and low. This is basic language, yet all except one student are sitting up or leaning forward in their seats to listen. The other student is leaning back, but still appears to be alert.

"We currently have sixty offenders on GPS. For the first felony offense for failure to register the sentence is two-years of GPS. For the second offense, it's five years." The brown-haired guest speaker pulls up a map on the screen. He accesses a specific client's case and shows the twenty-one students that person's whereabouts during the prior day. Those places are indicated on the map in green dots.

The electric shimmer flickers once.

GPS equipment is passed around the room from student to student. The one-piece unit is for a client's ankle. Students are told it charges for two hours per day and the man can make it buzz until the client calls him. It's about the size of half of a bulky remote control, black, and able to attach to a strap. The two-piece system is like a wristwatch, about two by three inches big. It links to a unit the size of a bulky cellphone. Both are black.

The men review cases. The mugshot of an offender is on the screen. He appears to be a white male. There is talk about child pornography, a parole violation, a twenty-seven-year sentence. "So that's Mr. Smith." The first man is matter of fact. Class is eerily quiet. The students' heads are up. For once, no one is scrolling on their phones.

The gray-haired man continues in his calm voice and manner. "I actually had a sexually violent predator here at this school." There is a soft "ooooh" from one of the students. The shimmer spikes. Some of the students are becoming restless.

The guest then discusses the need for supervised visits. Out chimes the first question from the class: "So even if they have a child that's underage, they have to be supervised?" The answer is yes.

"I had a client that had been in prison for twelve years, and once he got out, he friend-requested over two hundred Vietnamese children and tried to get them to send him pictures."

The electric current buzzes more strongly. Students shift in their chairs. The air is thick with uncomfortable silence.

The friendly gray-haired guest speaker begins to read a confession statement of a twenty-seven-year-old client. He matter-of-factly reads explicit information about the victim, using graphic terms, and incredibly vivid language.

The shimmer flickers highly around the room. There are outraged "what's?!" expressed by various students. The guest speaker provides descriptive details about the client's habits. The girl in front of her slowly shakes her head. The word "orgy" pops up along with pornographic descriptions. The students respond with "ughs" and "ewws."

"There is a significant reason I am reading this to you, it's not just for shock value," the guest speaker insists. "What the hell!" exclaims another student in response.

"How do you think he's doing on probation?" the gray-haired man asks.

The electric shimmer explodes into a cacophonous firework of sparks.

"He's not in jail?"—"He should be locked away if he did all that stuff!" Outrage. Anger. Disbelief.

"He's perfect. You know why? He's not drinking anymore." The guest speaker continues, kindly saying, "It's not our job to point fingers at these people, it's our job to help these people. There's a law enforcement aspect to our job, and there's a social work aspect to our job."

The slideshow switches to a slide about internship and volunteer information. Two students take pictures of the slide.

The guest speaker wraps up his presentation. Time has come for the class to end for the day. The slide show skips to the last slide and the screen goes black.

Class applauds.

The electric current has quieted back down. Students move on with their day.

Pizza Party

They're in a community room in a residence hall. Chairs are set up theater-style on the left side of the room. There is occasional seating and high-tops along the windows on the right side. It's music day. The class has left their assigned classroom and regularly scheduled programming for an enrichment activity. The instructor promises pizza for lunch.

Class begins with a lecture on music related to the subject of their learning community. The instructor is a musician himself. "I play string instruments. Mandolin, banjo, ukulele. Guitar is my main instrument. I can do some bass. Nothing with a bow." He passes out stapled sets of handouts. They are lyric sheets for the songs he is about to present. Two students whisper to each other once the presentation starts. The instructor admonishes them, saying, "Y'all please. I should be the only one talking right now." The students were looking at the lyric sheet together, presumably whispering on topic.

One of the video clips is Bob Marley's "I Shot the Sheriff." The instructor comments, "I don't think that smoke was a fog machine." There is no apparent reaction from the class to his comment, but a student in the back row is gently rocking to the music. Is this measurable student Engagement?

At the conclusion of the lecture portion of the enrichment event, the instructor breaks the class up into four groups of four students and one group of five students. The groups' task is to research songs with themes related to their major. They are asked to identify one song from each genre of country, rock, and rap. The class gets animated as the instructor goes around the room and assigns themes to each group. Students are sitting in groups on the occasional seating, each with electronic devices looking up things online. Compared to the noise level during the lecture portion of class, this buzz is rambunctious. Students appear to be excited about researching a connection between their major and popular culture.

In the back of the room, the catering staff is setting up pizza and sodas. Class seems unaware that food is in their near future.

The Peer Mentors' Tales

Nine peer mentors are gathered in a classroom with two learning community staff members and the learning community graduate student. It's mid-November and the mentors are asked to share their experiences working with learning community students this term.

Some of the peer mentors express their struggles with getting students to come to out-of-class events. "It wasn't, like, a bad semester . . . [It] taught me to connect with them on their level. I really enjoyed connecting with the students." Nevertheless, when he invited his students (who majored in health-related fields) to a blood pressure training event, only two from a class of twenty-plus students attended. He had tried his best to promote the event: in class, through a group text, and even in person as he ran into students in the [science] building. A second peer mentor concurred. She had tried all of his promotional methods and even included an event on the syllabus. Still, several students failed to attend. Neither of them appears frustrated. They are simply passing along the reality of it all.

Another peer mentor's experience was the opposite, maybe because she was in a learning community with sophomores. "Overall great experience," she begins. She explains that it was different from the previous year, because second-year students already know the resources. She was able to have deeper conversations with her students compared to the year before. She continues by saying, "What worked were personalized emails." She reports having repeat meetings that turned into one- and two-hour-long conversations. "I had a good time, and I think they did too." One of the learning community staff members asks if her conversations with students were about "mostly stuff in the classroom folks are struggling with." The peer mentor replies, "No, this was more the bigger picture, since they are closer to graduation."

Some of the peer mentors connected with their students more than others. One mentor shares that she recommended study groups to her community, and the GroupMe has been blowing up with them. In the beginning, her students thought of her as another instructor, but she pointed out to them that some of them were older than she was. It helped.

Others express that they didn't get a chance to adequately introduce themselves and their role at the beginning of the semester, stifling their interactions with their students from day one. The combination of this lack of introduction and out-of-class events not taking place until later in the semester made things more challenging. One peer mentor barely interacts with her community during class time. Another is gifted ten to fifteen minutes to address her group at the end of each class. A third asked her instructor for fifteen minutes to address her students during class time.

The range of experiences of these peer mentors is confounding. So much appears to depend on their own preferences, their instructor, and the combined personalities of the students in their communities. What is considered best practice tends to work for some peer mentors, but not all. They may have the same job description, but the lived experiences of their roles are heterogeneous.

The meeting ends with a staff member asking how the office could support peer mentors in the future. One of the mentors explains he was challenged by not having answers to basic questions, like where certain buildings are on campus. The graduate assistant replies, "So provide a campus map is what I'm hearing."

Laughter rings around the room.

Smith, Marx, and Engels

Today's topic of their morning learning community class is the economy. The instructor shares a personal example to explain an abstract concept.

Let me tell you this way. Last week I had to call the cable company. I get extremely nervous when I don't have an internet connection. First of all, I realize I'm talking to an entity far removed from this country, but I can understand him, so no problem there. And then I realize he's just googling stuff, which is the exact thing I'm doing. Reliance on another country for material goods is, to me, economically damaging.

Students are staring at the projection screen. A few are copying down what's on the display.

The instructor continues, *in 2010 the student loan companies really started pushing me to pay them. Used to be you could defer six months if you weren't ready, but now you're two days late and you start getting calls from 800 numbers from all over the country.*

A student mutters, "threatening to break your legs."

The instructor goes along with this comment, "the goon squad at the door with tire irons . . . I'm terrible at paying bills. I have enough money now, but I just don't keep up with it."

The instructor and that one student joke back and forth a few times. The rest of the class sits quietly in their individual desk chairs. A student in the back row is taking a drink from her white metal water bottle, checks something on her phone, and places the bottle back on the floor. She takes down the notes on the next slide.

The topic: Capitalism. The instructor jokes, "I'm getting ready to buy a phone; it's $1,200. I could get a car that's drivable for $1,200." He breezes through the PowerPoint. This isn't review, but he moves quickly. Perhaps there's a test coming up soon. Perhaps he teaches the same content in another section and wants to catch up.

To explain the concept of monopoly, the instructor asks, "Who do you go to for power in this state? The power company, right?" The class appears to have no idea. They are first-year students and most of them live on campus. She doubts many of them have ever paid a power bill.

They move on to socialism. The instructor explains, *we hear a lot these days about how capitalism is evil, but I encourage you to think about it as more complex*. He adds, *socialism is not the answer because it fails because of human greed*. He provides a complex example of human greed from another country. It's a lot to take in in a short amount of time.

"You're college students, I don't know what your bank account looks like, but it's likely not that thick."

By 10:35, an hour into a seventy-five-minute class, the instructor has gotten to the point in the PowerPoint at which he wants to stop. Students pack up their notebooks and take out their phones.

"I will make the quiz results available. You all did quite well."

One student plugs her laptop in the back of the room. Nobody leaves. Their second learning community class will start soon in this same classroom.

Start-istics

It is eight in the morning on the second day of class; we are still in the first week. He tells the class, a roughly ninety-student lecture class, that two or three students are allowed to use laptops—all other students must put theirs away. He permits laptop use for students working with the accessibility office only. Four people haven't yet registered for the textbook publisher's online quiz website that this class will use as a part of students' overall grade, and two students have yet to look at the course Blackboard site. He suggests they remedy this and that this is not a good way to start the course. He gives a few syllabus updates. He mentions there is a possible hurricane coming. The class rumbles at this; a buzz circulates throughout the room. Firmly yet gently he asks the class to quiet down, and they do.

He displays the first slide. It's a basic title template slide with a white background and black font, Helvetica maybe. Most students show signs of paying attention—taking notes (by hand), eyes forward. There is a yawn or two. That's understandable.

At 8:05 a.m., there is a knock at the back door. A student in the back row jumps up to open the door. A single late student walks in. The late student says something, but the words dissipate by the time they hit her ears. The instructor stops the lecture and turns to address her: "Hey, how's it going?" He continues the lecture.

He asks the class to define social science. From the audience, a definition tumbles out: "the study of social systems." He prods the class for more, as "you can't just define something with the same word." The same student adds more words but different ones. "Yes," he says emphatically. He asks a follow-up question, and another student on the opposite side of the room responds. He is one of five students—maybe ten students—who raised their hands.

Ten minutes later, a footer on a slide appears: "©McGraw-Hill Education."

Thirty minutes past this, students settle into their seats. The vibe is a bit more subdued. A student sits upright with his eyes closed and head resting in hand. She can see a side conversation, but she can't hear it. What does Engagement look like? Does it look like anything?

Postgraduation Employment Options

Two learning communities take a class trip to the zoo to see class concepts alive in the world. On one such trip, the class pauses at the brown bear exhibit and waits for a few minutes to see if a bear will come out of its house. There's a zookeeper placing food in the exhibit while the bears are locked away. One student jokes, pointing at the zookeeper: "Everyone wave! Oh, look at this one, that's crazy."

The faculty leader has the group move along when a bear doesn't appear once the zookeeper has left. Just as they have moved on, a bear comes out. She takes off her invisibility cloak and says, "There he is!" Several students come back to the bear enclosure, uttering *oohs* and *awwws*. Then a second bear comes out to feed.

The instructor explains another job option for students in his field of study. *Another possible job—I always relate things—is park ranger.*

As they move down the path to the next exhibit, the instructor overhears two students talking about what to do after they graduate. They are first-year students. "I just want to hurry up and graduate and start a career," expresses one student. Another asks, "What do you want to do?" The first student replies, "Like a government agency or Air Force." The second student reacts, "I just want to be a cop." The first student replies, "I don't wanna be a cop."

Origin Story, Part I

How did you decide to sign up for your learning community? "So, the learning community . . . I initially was going to do the residential learning community, but I require special housing accommodations that they couldn't accommodate in the residential learning community. And I did hear about it . . . There was a [major] day that my [high school] that a lot of people were from a technical center went to. [Advisor] came and it was just like, you know, we have [residential and nonresidential learning communities], you know, you guys should really look into these."

She was expecting to hear a story about orientation. She observed some aspects of orientation this year and was familiar with all the work put in by program coordinators and advisors to promote learning communities to students and get them registered. His origin story starts in high school though? "So [advisor] came to your high school?"

Almost. "The high schools brought us to [our advisor]." She attended a fair for his field of study that was held at one of the extension sites of this university closer to where he is from.

> I initially was in [field of study] but then [orientation] came and then they were like, oh, I want to teach. And they're like, 'there's no money in that you should do something else.' I'm like, okay, I'm just gonna, and then, you know, they gave me a breakdown of some of the other classes. And I'm like, I really want to take Accounting III for my [field of study] degree. And then I actually switched and then I caught [advisor] walking out the webinar like yeah so you told me I could switch right. I'm like, It's time. It's time to do that. So, we had a phone call the next day and she was like, 'yeah, I can switch you over just fine. Just out of curiosity, we do have room in the, still have room in the [learning community]. Do you want to join that?' and then I said, yes. And then you know, I talked to some other people. And then there was a little bit of a communication breakdown, too, because so my friends got the scholarship and they're actually required to be in the [learning community] so they didn't know that. And then I think it just slipped through the cracks. So, you know, it was me telling about them and I kind of drew them back into the [learning community] too . . .

Student Success

No cellphones in class. No laptops without permission. The door will be locked once class commences. Arriving ten minutes late is an absence. More than two absences result in a failing grade.

There are free planners for students to take in the student union building. There will be guest speakers to help students explore postgraduation jobs. There is a peer mentor who can arrange additional study sessions.

"This class is not meant to be difficult for you, it's meant to help you," the instructor exclaims.

The hushed conversations in the back row and the student scrolling on his phone appear to betray the students' indifference. Or maybe this is simply the behavior they are used to from high school. After all, senior year ended less than six months ago for most (but not all) of these students. They are now faced with new expectations, new rules, and new opportunities.

When asked who already feels overwhelmed, several of the students raise their hands and grumble.

This is day one.

On the Hunt

We begin our hunt for student engagement indicators with multiple quivers in our arsenal. Eyes sharp as those of an eagle, ready to see color, smiles, frowns, spaces, and Chick-Fil-A cups. Ears tuned to capture silence, murmurs, noise, buzz, and speech. Fingers limbered up for typing, writing, and taking photographs. Minds opened to perceive active involvement in classroom learning,[9] a sense of peer belonging,[10] and a safe and supportive place to learn[11] but also disruptive student behavior, resistance to learning, and student-faculty conflict.[12]

Everything is fair game: to be gathered like wild berries and mushrooms and to be reviewed in weekly intervals. Our actors both stay the same and undergo change. So do we. Yet we faithfully attempt to capture that which is before us, always already aware that we seek the imperceptible. We also know that capture is incommensurate with our re/valuing of the ordinary; anecdotes cannot become the next structuring devices. Those anecdotes we narrate will provide an imperfect glimpse at the ordinary impacts of learning communities.

More Engaged

Um, I think the students were really engaged. One of the things I observed just, I taught two, I taught, I taught two sections of that course . . . One was [a learning community section of this three-credit course], the other wasn't. I think the students who are in my [learning community] section were more engaged maybe because they knew that they were part of the program, the [learning community] program. And so, they were more conscious of the fact that they were being monitored. Mmm. That probably, you know, had a positive impact on them. But they're way more engaged than the other class. I can tell that, yeah, they were more engaged than the other class. They asked a lot more questions, and they did, and they actually did better on assignments and the exams.

What exactly does *more engaged* look like?

Oh, so there were times I talked to them about the other courses that were part of the [learning community] just to understand what they were experiencing or going through and you know, they told me stuff like, well right after my class they had [their other three-credit learning community course] . . . So, I think that that in effect influenced their participation in my course, because they knew they had to take another class as part of the [learning community]. And there was probably one before mine and then one after mine. So just knowing that there was this focus on them, you know, and that there was the expectation that they will do well in [their learning community] or just knowing that there was a program called the [learning communities program] and that they were sort of like part of that I think make them to be more engaged. I think they asked more questions in class, but I also, if you recall, because you were in several of the classes, I also asked them a lot of questions and I think that I got good responses from the class. Because they were, they were, they were prepared. I think they read . . . assigned chapters before class and they were ready to answer the questions that I had. Of course, there was a few people who asked me questions, but I also asked them questions just to be sure that they were following, you know, what I was saying and that they had actually done the reading before class. So that's how I would answer that question?

Temporal Student Engagements

She had a good conversation with a trusted participant.

I don't know if you ever feel this way or maybe in the past have felt this way. I'm like, now in my midtwenties. I'm like, wow, if I knew what I knew now when I was 18 like I'd have a different major. I have a different, like my life would be totally different. Right. And it's like okay but I'm 18 [they laugh]. And being able to kind of like, like think about that and I think it's a hard work because it's one of those like this can be a really great tool that if you use when you're graduating when you're twenty-two, you're going to be really happy you did it, but like, why do it now?

She laughs. She can't hold back her own experiences.
"Right, yeah. No. I used to just tell people when I was an advisor that, like I never knew what engineering meant. Like I had no context for the word."
She laughs again. This makes her look dumb, but oh well. She was. Whatever that means here. Was she dumb? Was the university not engaging her?
"So, I changed my major five times as an undergrad, but like when I came in, I was weirdly obsessed with traffic patterns. This gets too nerdy quick. And I didn't know what engineering was, like traffic engineering, like civil . . . had I known and maybe had a little bit more aptitude in crucial subjects. I could have been some bomb ass engineer. I don't know."

Buzz

The instructor asks the class: "What are middle-class values? Can someone give me an example of middle-class values?"

A student who brings no notebook, no computer, no bag of any kind to class jumps right in. He paints a picture for the class of a complete suburban landscape, including a picket fence, two kids, a dog . . . ending with "a push lawnmower, that's important."

A spark flies around the room. A student in the front row picks it up and goes next: this family's kid is student government president.

Another spark, another student, this time from the middle left of the room: "college education."

The instructor jumps back in: "I'll give you a few more, individual responsibility . . . the ability to express yourself verbally and in writing . . ."

And the igniter of the initial spark jumps right back in: "Are we talking about America specifically? In a lot of middle-class values, monogamy is a value."

While the instructor keeps listing values, the spark has turned into a buzz. The buzz volume is high and has been ever since the word *monogamy* pierced the room. The student who takes no notes chuckles and utters a low "Jeffrey Epstein" that breaks through the buzz. She wrinkles her nose. Many side conversations are happening.

A student asks the instructor a question about how these values came to stick. The buzz continues. In about ten minutes it fades to just one or two low side conversations happening, no words audible . . . and then it dies out completely.

Competing Priorities

Learning Communities, a program to Engage students. Learning Communities, a program to bring students into your college's majors. Learning Communities, a program to generate revenue for your college by having more students in your college taking more credit hours in your college. Learning Communities, a program to promote student Engagement and generate enrollment in specific corners of the university.

> So, we did this like report of major changes like who, you know, left and, and I think so there was one day it was like the end of the semester, and we were talking about this parallel plan and, you know, this . . . one of the assignments the students have to select another major that they would be there parallel plan. And I remember this girl who wants to be an [job title]

who's currently majoring in [field of study A]. She was like, well, my parallel major's [field of study B]. And I was like, why, and she was like, because I realized I can have this job with any major and [field of study C] is just as - could, I could also do. And I was like, boom, like let's, let's take this apart.

They both laugh.

And also, like, similarly, we had a bunch of students that wanted to do [field of study D]. Which is always very interesting my end all goal if we were to continue this like two, three years out, would be to have a learning community like with the [related college] and get through all of the like [similar major] students because it's kind of confusing because the [field of study D] doctoral program is in the [college], but like [field of study E], is not. And I think we sometimes, kind of like, are like because of [field of study D] we put them into this pool that I don't know is the best. So like . . . out of those four students every single one of them changed their major.

She laughs. "Whoops."

Lecture Format

The instructor, in the middle of lecturing, cues to a previous lecture: "Does anyone remember what I said about [these] theories?"

A student in the back responds. His voice is too low for her to make out words, but the instructor does: "Good, I'm glad you remember."

This student has the publisher PowerPoint slides up on his laptop screen most or all of each class. He is able to give these types of quick definitional responses in each class. He gets credit for remembering, credit for publisher notes, and credit for the practices of lecture format.

A student who sits with his book open at the front of the room gets up to leave early. He seems to have precleared this with the instructor. The instructor pauses class for just a bit, and then the lecture format keeps plugging away. This packing up doesn't prompt viral packing as it does in other classes because of the "high school" back-to-back scheduling of these two learning community classes. Or maybe because of something else.

A sneeze punctures the lecture format halfway through class. The sound of "bless you" rises from corners of the class that infrequently speak.

Toward the end of class, the instructor asks for the four components of a theory. A student in the back right of the room who always has her book out lists each component in sequence, without pause. The instructor lists them on the board as she talks. The instructor then asks for the definition of the first component. She speaks up again to give the definition, seamlessly. This is a rolling through of lecture format, rolling along, seamless, without friction, content from the instructor, from students, from the publisher, through lecture slides and books, mediated flow.

Quiz Anxiety

You guys made me really nervous last night. It was like 11:15 p.m., and there were still empty spaces in the gradebook. I was hoping you would get the quiz in there. One student made me really nervous, I even texted him. I looked up his number in the student information system and realized I already had it in my phone.

Body without Organs

It is field trip day.[13] One by one, students file into the room and put their backpacks and bags on a wire shelf near the entrance of the room. Slowly, they gather in a semicircle around the metal table in the middle of the room. There is a large zipped black bag on top of the table. It's clear there is something inside the bag. This day has been a long time coming. A frisson of electricity jumps from student to student, erratically connecting all that are present.

The room has worktables against two of the walls, shelves with plastic displays at the far-right corner. There are several green five-gallon buckets on a shelf. She wonders what they contain. There are no labels. The room has a chill. A few students have hands in their jacket pockets.

The guest speaker is a petite blond woman wearing a little black dress. She explains some procedural items as she dons pink rubber gloves.

Students are super quiet and pay rapt attention to her words. Per her instructions, there are no cellphones out. Honestly, it's a first this term.

The guest speaker offers students a last chance to leave the room before she unzips the bag. One student takes her up on her offer, perhaps to leave for another class. Perhaps to get the hell away from what is about to happen next. Then it begins. The woman unzips the bag and pulls out certain "structures." It is a body. The body of a ninety-one-year-old female.

Record scratch.

The speaker describes the process of embalming and the fact that this body is completely drained of blood. She has also been heavily dissected and looks nothing like bodies on TV crime dramas. Her flesh is a brownish color, and her texture is somewhere between a cooked hot dog and tree bark. Three more students leave.

One student is holding her nose. There is a faint smell, but she doesn't know how to describe it. Maybe it smells like turpentine? Maybe it smells like decay? How would she know?

"Here are the intestines," the speaker says, holding them up. There are "wows" from several students. She does the same with the detached rib cage. It does not look like she envisioned. It looks like a shrunken, brownish piece of something. A shriveled baseball mitt.

She stays toward the back of the room with her back pressed into the wall of lockers by the exit. She spots a trashcan and wonders if it would be inappropriate to use it if she gets sick.

Students ask to see the body's face and one student asks whether the eyes are still in the body's head. The speaker asks, "you want to see her face?" and lifts the sheet that covers her head. There are *awwws* from the students. They are crowding around the table, careful not to touch anything. They are engrossed. Are they Engaged? If so, is it the Engagement the university administration is looking for, the kind whose residue clings to a survey administered in a few months or a few years?

Ordinary Fidgets

A side conversation among students is happening across the room.

A whisper is shared between friends behind her. It is probably inaudible to others in class.

A student responds to a quick question from the instructor that is audible to others in the class. The sounds from students die out again.

The student buzz in the room from five minutes before class started is now nowhere to be felt twenty minutes in.

A buzz ebbs and flows as the instructor discusses funeral rituals.

A four-person conversation starts up a row in from of her. These students have their notebooks out, but their pens and pencils are resting on their desk. One pen is up and moving. A student is between conversations, the one with her friends and the one-sided conversation of lecture. The conversation among friends is now down to just two friends.

Another student fidgets with a pen.

A student rests their chin on a desk. The student's eyes are wide open, and they are looking straight ahead.

Thirty minutes into class, there are now five students with their heads on their desk, including the same woman as before.

A student has their institutionally branded planner out.

There are now six heads on desks. The original woman is still one of them, though her eyes are now open.

Forty minutes into class, the instructor asks another quick question to the room, this time a nod to integrative learning: "All of you are taking [paired course,] right? Tell me what [concept] is then, in [paired course]?" A student responds, quickly. The instructor affirms the response and continues lecturing.

A buzz rolls around the room, but she isn't quite sure what its spark was. It goes away as quickly as it came.

A few students are still holding their pens in their hands, up and ready, all set for the next quotable quote or notable note. Many pens are laying on desks instead. One pen is still the object of a student's fidgeting.

The original woman with her head on her desk today is now up! She lets out a big yawn. She now plays with a pen out on her desk also. She crosses her arms on her desk and looks down, then looks out.

What is the story of this room? This class? This aggregation of individuals?

There are notable moments of buzz in the next fifteen minutes of class. They come strong and then die back, only to erupt again.

One hour and eight minutes into class, with only seven minutes left, no one has started to pack up. Our OG sleeper is even taking notes! Lecture continues, the slides keep sliding along, and students are taking notes in a similar pattern as they were at prior moments in class. Most students have notes out, and about half are actively taking notes at any given point.

There are side conversations happening in places. A four-way conversation is now a five-way conversation.

Four minutes left in class. There is now a laptop open in the back of this no technology allowed class.

The sounds of packing up are spreading. The sound of a three-ring binder opening and closing. Backpacks rustling. The instructor is still lecturing—and now he ends. Class ends three minutes early. Fluid sounds of packing up spike when he says "thank you"—it's the first confirmation that class is ending, a format that all understand.

Clusters of students walk toward the back doors and leave class together. "Where are you going?"

There is a meeting of friends-of-friends on the walk out of class. "Nice to meet you." They exchange a handshake.

One student walks against the flow of students to the front of the room. She has something to ask the instructor. "When you were talking about cultures, I really wanted you to talk about cultural appropriation." The instructor promises to do this first thing next class. He asks the student to bring it up.

Ordinary Impact

In and through this collection of anecdotes, we produce the beginning of an ordinary impact, impasses from which student and institutional outcomes may emerge—or not.[14] The book moves in waves and flows across the micro-moments of student Engagement and Integrative Learning within learning communities. From rooms full of first-year students ready to learn at 8:00 a.m., Chick-fil-A chicken biscuits and Starbucks pink drinks in hand, to Zoom rooms of muted faces, "fuck this learning community," and all the spaces in-between. From publisher slides to notetaking in a plain text editor to cameras off to walking in late and being called out to sleeping in class sitting upright to sleeping in class in bed with a companion alongside to watching cell-phone videos to watching subtitled reality television shows to doing who knows what in Zoom life to responding to questions in small phrases to lecture format to being locked out of a lecture hall for being late to being locked out of Zoom for being late to overwhelming boredom to cadaver labs to lit chat boxes to raised hands to heads on desks into the first semester of student possibilities at this university and back out again to the still life that has crystallized around it. Student Engagement comes into focus by the last day of classes, or by the National Survey of Student Engagement (NSSE) administration date; Integrative Learning comes into focus with the coordinating office's Learning Community Design Canvas or the AAC&U's rubric;[15] high-impact comes into focus with next year's retention metric and four years later with the calculation of an on-time graduation rate. The anecdotes of classroom life remain in the impasse, out-of-focus, opaque.[16]

Buzz

Students still make the sounds of getting ready: papers moving about, backpacks up and down from table to floor and back, pens, laptops being readied. A few students respond to the instructor's question—the words are indistinguishable from the buzz.

The instructor shows a long video.

The slides return, the instructor pulls up a website. Student buzz ebbs and flows. A louder conversation happens in the back, then fades away.

You Get a Point, and You Get a Point

What did student engagement in your course look like this past term?

> . . . Um, I think a lot of the highlights were a little bit more some of like the success or the major changes or some of those more epiphanies. To be completely like candid, it's not that I don't view some of the assignments in my class . . . necessary. But there are some that I don't . . . that again is for that bigger picture thinking. So, for example, like their résumé assignment. Like, it's important to have, right? And that's why we do it. And it's important to know that Career Resources is a, or, Career Services, excuse me, is a resource that we have on campus and things like that. But it's, sometimes I kind of view my class and more like Oprah. Like 'you get a point and you get a point and you get a point,' like, come on . . . and I mean I tell all of them very much on the first day, if you meet me I will meet you. Like this is honestly supposed to help you grow and do things more, I tend to be like a pretty lenient

professor . . . So, it's tough for me sometimes, because it's like, I don't really look at the grades. I don't look at the completion of the assignments and things like that. I look more at what is the student . . . are they putting in a little bit of effort? Are they having the conversations? Are they thinking more big picture about all of this? So, it's kinda tough.

They're Just Not About It

One of the communities she observed this term seemed to have strange boundaries around what constituted the courses in the community. Learning communities here comprise two three-credit courses and one paired major-specific one-credit course. She knew what these three courses were listed as on paper, and she observed two of them every week (mostly) throughout the term. But during this time, she kept hearing about a fourth course discussed as if it were in the learning community. Many, but not all, students in the learning community were also taking this fourth class. She asked around—why was there a shadow quasi-learning community course in this learning community? A few folks were willing to talk with her more about this. All expressed variations of the following:

"I'm also going to be honest, I think that it's low hanging, oh god this is going to be bad."

She laughs.

"So, I think this past year, in particular, in 2019 we got a lot of pressure from [the central learning community coordinating office] to have an overarching assignment, to have there be cross collaboration among the classes, particularly in terms of an assignment."

She pauses.

"I think [one of the courses formally in the learning community] is just . . . [that] department doesn't really care if they teach in a learning community or not. I don't think like, I think they kind of enjoy it but like they don't, they're scientists, they don't care about the like engagement . . . like no. Like they're just not about it. So I think it was more low hanging fruit for the [fourth, quasi-learning community course] and the [other course formally in the learning community] and I mean there they are . . . there's a lot in common [between them] . . . So, I think it was a little bit of a low hanging fruit as well for them to kind of connect in their assignments."

First Day, Take Two

Same community, different day, different learning community class. Students file into the classroom quietly. This room is set up with tables and a center aisle. The instructor has already arrived. He asks, "How is everyone doing?" Students give a few affirmative murmurs and head nods. She takes this to mean that this will be another quiet class. The instructor asks who remembers seeing him at orientation this past summer. Most students give acknowledging head bops. One student says she does not. He walks up to her desk and says, "Hi there, I'm your advisor!" He shakes her hand. There is some chatter among students. The vibe is different here; it's a comfortable, relaxed atmosphere. Maybe because this is a one-credit major-related class.

Ten minutes after class starts, students are still arriving. Is this a first day of class problem? Only time will tell. The instructor asks the peer mentor to introduce himself. He is a star student: a senior, graduating this term, president of an honor society, a research assistant on campus, already admitted to graduate school. Students are taking this in. Will his accolades help them connect with him in a meaningful way? Will it help them be more Engaged in their chosen major or even in this learning community? What would that Engagement look like?

After this introduction comes the standard review of the syllabus and term calendar. An icebreaker activity, two truths and a lie, takes the remainder of class time. The instructor leads the way, sharing two statements that are true about himself, and one that's not. Immediately, an animated debate ensues among the students over which of his three statements is the lie. She is taken aback by the intensity of conversation that seems to come out of nowhere. Students are speaking on top of each other, the buzz reaching new heights with each person that goes next. One student says, "I sold drugs in school" and the class responds with laughter, followed by discussion and more laughter. At the end, she isn't sure whether that was in fact the lie or one of his truths. Another student says she has been crying herself to sleep every night because she wants to go home, and this is one of her truths. The class responds with supportive comments.

Is this the beginning of community?

Impact

I think we sometimes get in this, like, do we do this, you do this
to this is this do this. And I think, again, if I'm a little biased,

it's kind of like we already had this well-oiled machine that we obviously do want to make better in different ways, but maybe not in the ways that kind of like [central learning community coordinating office] wants. Like I think [the coordinating office] sometimes is stuck in this like 'theory to practice' way and something for example from the main meeting: We were even told to, like, 'Okay, think back to an assignment that you had that made the most meaningful,' you know, 'that was really meaningful for you and your collegiate experience.' And like a coordinating office staff member got up there, even in talked about an assignment that she had done. And I think where I struggle sometimes with the overall kind of theory and goals and this is how you make . . . this is how it's impactful, I think it sometimes struggles to translate to certain [State U.] learning communities and particularly ours because a lot of those more impactful things are things that tend to happen junior, senior year when students are within a major.

. . . And so it's one of those like, I don't disagree with what the theory says with examples and, and experiences that students can have, but I can't provide that to an 18-year-old that still swipes into the back of the classroom 15 weeks into like and . . . I hate it, but it's like the, the caliber of student at [State U.], particularly in their first semester, cannot handle . . . like they are not at that level. Like, we have to get them to figure out, quite honestly, like so, every year at orientation or . . . whatever we're calling it these days, we ask what are the top five differences between college and high school. And like we ask them, how much did you study, do you study outside of the classroom in high school and usually like 90 percent of them say never. Like we have to get them to figure out how to study and what studying is and what life outside of the classroom is before we can even get them to do this really big great impactful thing. And I'm not saying that they can't ever get there, but it's like that . . . What I would change is almost, like, how to measure what this impact, like with the question that you asked before, like how are we measuring this impact? Like, I think that sometimes the coordinating office in terms of like [another coordinating office program linked to Kuh's high-impact practices][17] and, and, learning communities and all these things, they think about they want. Like I almost view it as like they want to produce this like, like a commercial, right? Like this great website and this great like look at what these students are doing. And we're so great. And we're so great. And realistically, a lot of the learning communities like aren't commercial, like, producible experiences. Does that make sense? Like we have a student in our learning community that attended [State U.] for her first semester. She was admitted into another institution's major-specific program in January and she left [State U.] and she went. She had a 4.0 first semester. She's going into a job connected to this major, like, she's doing great things. How, like to coordinating office standards, that's probably not success. Like, who am I to say otherwise. Does that make sense?

Absolutely. She thinks about the inadequacies of metrics and other structuring devices in higher education all the time. She feels the point being made here deep in her soul.

"And so, I think that that's kind of something that I would change. It's just this like this mindset of how first-year students can be fit into this conversation and do really great things, but just as a first-year student, particularly with the type of students that we have at [State U.] I like we're not we're not [a selective university] We're not a Harvard. Like we're not this picture perfect first-year student, so, yeah."

She laughs.

"Sorry."

A twist. Does she still agree?

Imperceptible Impacts

Virtually every actor at a college or university is interested in the college experience being a positive one for students. This desire gets expressed in many ways. The concept of college impact as quantifiable and machine computable has been around since at least the late 1960s and the early work of Alexander Astin.[18] The idea of college as a place for the general progress of students, and relatedly communities, long predates this.[19] The concept of impact is one of progress. Impact is movement, difference, a shift from inertia, value-added. But progress and impact, as a machine computable thing, have only become interchangeable in the last fifty years. To what effect?

Machine-computable impact is the making-perceptible of progress. Measurement is the making-perceptible of progress. This is how researchers and practitioners in higher education now feel comfortable making statements about what we know about higher education. Data is the standard of truth; all other forms of knowledge become anecdote. Impact attunes progress to perceptibility.

Progress is never fully perceptible. This is evident across domains and theoretical traditions, from student progress in college classrooms to faculty progress in college classrooms, staff progress through professional development, even to student progress on athletic fields.[20] Measurements like grades, student evaluation scores, and runs batted in say something about a person's progress, sure. However, in very important ways, progress is imperceptible.[21] We are generally unaware of the point when concepts click within ourselves or in others. We cannot perceive the effect of reading one more chapter of a book. Others cannot measure the impact of being late to class just that one time in the seventh week, because the night was long, and that class starts way too early. If progress at some point can be measured, these ordinary points must too be part of this. And yet on their own, the imperceptibility of an occurrence like walking into class late with coffee in hand, or the ordinariness of murmurs of student buzz that emerge when a particular student starts speaking, renders them insignificant. Their imperceptibility devalues them in a world of outcomes and analytics. When this happens, at least two dangers emerge.

First, when we do not value imperceptible progress, our colorful worlds recede to black and white. Imperceptible progress is the texture of student experience. Losing some of the opportunities for these moments of imperceptible progress is part of the loss campus denizens feel in the extended nightmare of the COVID-19 pandemic. These moments are not *just* anecdotes or insignificant ordinary moments.[22] *They are progress; they are impact.*

Second, if we cannot attune to anecdotes as impact in all of their imperceptibility,[23] we do as we do now. We engage in a decades-long assessment, then completion movement now under the banner of student success wherein we empty the contents of progress by reverse-engineering the student experience for perceptible progress. *We focus on the making-perceptible instead of progress; we conflate making-perceptible with impact.*

To take the affective dimensions of student engagement seriously is to experience student engagement as potential that becomes reality as well as potential that hangs in the balance, waiting for its time to come—and not knowing the difference between the two. To value affect is also to experience integrative learning as the concrete connections among linked courses and the innumerable perceptible and imperceptible entanglements that linked courses produce. Affect comprises the impasse, the space and time where one outcome might become another—or become nothing at all.[24] Affect constitutes the space prior to which students become individualized and measurable. Affect provides a means of valuing learning communities and other university spaces in excess of impact, high, low, or otherwise.[25]

Debrief

The instructor waits for her in the hallway outside of the classroom. Here we go. She has a feeling the instructor is going to complain about her students, and she doesn't want to be a party to it. The instructor starts by saying "there are some very immature people in this class." Not sure how to respond, she smiles and says, "well, they are fresh out of high school." The instructor insists. "I teach freshmen at 10:00 a.m. as well and it's like night and day. It's a real group mentality with this class." This instructor is teaching learning community students for the first time this term. Is she unaware that a sense of community and students helping each other are two of the goals of learning communities at this institution? Or perhaps she knows but finds this aspect particularly challenging. Are there avenues for faculty to debrief in other forums?

It is uncomfortable as they walk out together. There is an awkward silence from which she can't escape. Students helping each other—surely, this a piece of cultivating a learning community culture. She remembers reading about some of the less pleasant side effects of learning communities, such as disruptive student behavior.[26] She hasn't noticed this in the other classes she is observing this term and can't help but wonder to what degree this is an insurmountable problem.

Origin Story, Part II

How did the students of this learning community come to know their instructor was part Asian?

"I'm part Asian, but that doesn't mean I was born knowing how to use chopsticks."

Buzz pops up immediately. The instructor launches into story time. The gist: he learned how to use chopsticks in San Francisco while at a conference. It was two in the morning, and he found himself at a Vietnamese restaurant in "desperate need" of food and without a fork in sight.

This is a notable instance of the instructor sharing something personal, and something personal that is related to the class topic. There is a crack in lecture format today. The buzz in the room is both on and off topic. His story has jolted energy into the room, and that energy has spawned a few side conversations.

Why Are All the White Kids Sitting Together in the Cafeteria?

At lunch time,[27] the class waits outside a restaurant-style cafeteria at the field trip site. Students are seated outside the dining hall around picnic tables while they wait to go in. Other visitors stroll by, enjoying the unusually warm fall day. Finally, the doors open and students file inside to line up to get pizza. There are two stacks of four to five pizza boxes with pepperoni and cheese pizza as options. Next to the pizza boxes are rows of Sprite, Coke, and Diet Coke cans.

One student cuts in line to grab a slice with pepperoni and then belatedly looks for a plate. Everyone else is in line, following the expected etiquette. After a few moments, a pizza box empties and the student who grabbed the last slice moves away to sit down. "At least have the decency to move the empty box," the student behind him grumbles.

More than two-thirds of students in this class are Black. Four out of the six white students have self-selected to sit in a booth together. The rest of the class is seated in five additional booths. She's not sure what to make of this segregated seating arrangement but it rankles her. For the majority of this field trip, the foursome has walked together in a group. They sit in proximity during class as well.

The instructor encourages the students to grab more pizza and drinks several times. Finally, it's time to move on.

Chapter Two

Change (2019–20)

Swipe Up, Swipe Down

She takes her seat in the lecture hall at 7:55 a.m., aware in her bones that it's too early for any of this, yet here we all are. Almost three months of this feeling twice a week. She looks up to see who else is here in the room, what the spirit is, and if there's anything to attend to. She sees a familiar sight. A student walks in at 8 a.m., itself a perilous action in this room. Instead of hurrying to his seat, he moves to the black box installed on the wall next to the door, takes out his university ID card, and swipes it in a card reader that is part of the box. He swipes up and down to sign in and promptly turns around and walks to his usual seat. As soon as he sits down, the instructor walks up the center aisle of the lecture hall and gives each person to his left and right an attendance sheet. One blank piece of paper is passed down each row on each side of the room for students to sign their name and pass to the outside. This practice has been ongoing twice a week for almost three months.

A Lesson

"Survival of the fittest means 'I take what I want' . . . that's the way the animal kingdom works. As humans we came together after many wars and decided we wouldn't act like animals." The instructor's example continues. *We will regress as humans without social contracts. A lion is in a pride, one male and many females. He keeps the other males away and protects his females and kids. Other males think to attack each other to steal their pride. If one wins over another, he takes over the other's pride, kills all of the cubs so that he does not have to take care of the other male's kids, and he has his own kids with the other's females. This is how lions work—how animal communities work. We cannot do this as humans.*

I am average height and weight. Every guy in this class is stronger than me. I would not make it. We need a social contract for order, or we act like lions or animals.

The Starting Line-Up

She takes a seat in the back corner of the darkened classroom with the attempt to hide. The lights are turned off, and the projector is on, but no presentation is pulled up on the screen. The instructor and peer mentor acknowledge her on her way into the class. The students do not. The room is packed to the gills with students waiting for their second learning community class this week to begin. Hardly any seats are vacant. She can feel their anxiety. Uncertainty. Uneasiness. How will this class go for them? Will the instructor welcome them with the empathy they so clearly need bestowed upon them? Or will she stay on topic and on task like their first instructor did?

As it turns out, this class may be different. Maybe this is because this class is the one-credit 'introduction to your major and the university' class that undoubtedly not many of them think they need. This class, unlike their lecture-based classes, only meets once a week for fifty minutes. This class, along with its instructor, is an extension of their summer orientation program. The instructor will be the students' academic advisor for as long as they pursue this major. And she appears to be friendly.

The instructor calls class to order with a wide smile on her face. It's a captivating departure from the instructor of yesterday's lecture course. The peer mentor's cellphone is being passed around the room from student to student. They are encouraged to add their phone numbers to GroupMe, a group chat app that the community will be using to communicate informally. The phone is followed by a printed roster. Students are asked to initial their names to confirm attendance. A stack of syllabi, a major-specific information sheet, and a flyer for a job opportunity for their field of study follow the first two items. It's a busy first five minutes of class. The rustle of papers, binders, bookbags, and the shuffle of pens, cellphones, and notebooks appear like the carelessly choreographed movements of a first-time dance troupe.

"You are a family. You're members of a family."

A beat.

Out of cacophony, silence.

This is the first time something approaching *community* has been referenced outside of the academic connection of linked classes. The twenty-four students seem nonplussed. There is no reaction reflected on their faces. If this is news to them, they aren't letting on. She is unable to tell whether they welcome this idea or not. They appear to be paying rapt attention, but their faces are as yet expressionless.

The instructor moves on with introductions of herself and the peer mentor and class continues. We've just left the starting line.

"The Furniture We Are Forever Rearranging"

"I feel like the [central learning community coordinating office] has done a lot of research on these kinds of [learning communities]. I think they've done a lot more theory, like this is more theory based. And that they—"

She pauses. Is she collecting her thoughts? Filtering her thoughts?

"—are struggling with, like the 'to practice' space. I hate to say like we're biased because we do it well. But I think it is kind of one of those things that they're trying to honestly help and give ideas of things to maybe people that need it more. They're trying to help with recruitment and help with these things because some of the learning communities are struggling."[1]

A Carrot but No Stick

It is the summer. Learning community faculty are asked to gather for two ninety-minute workshops to help prepare them for teaching learning communities in the fall. Their reward for attendance is payment of the first half of their faculty stipend.

During the workshop,

- faculty are going to be asked to add a common learning community statement to their syllabi;

- faculty will be advised they may end up teaching their learning community courses online and need to design their courses with that in mind; and

- faculty will need to incorporate at least one integrated assignment into their learning communities.

The workshop facilitator is cautious about how to proceed. "I can tell them to sign onto Zoom with their institutional email, but I don't want to confuse or frustrate them even more. I know they are already frustrated." After the workshop,

- faculty will be asked to complete a workshop evaluation survey;

- faculty who complete the survey will then be emailed their homework assignment; and

- faculty will need to complete this homework prior to the second day of the workshop.

The facilitator is hopeful faculty will complete these tasks. "Surely they'll do it. They're adults." One of her teammates is less certain. "The 80/20 rule will come into play. 80 percent of them will do, 20 percent won't."

A Student's Definition of a Learning Community

She is curious about what students thought they were getting themselves into when signing up for a learning community at State U. What were they told during orientation by their advisors? How did their parents explain the benefits? How did the students make sense of all this information? A first-generation student explains:

My understanding was that I would be put in classes with a group of other first-time freshmen students who were intended [field of study] majors. We would be put in the same classroom. That way we could develop this group and we could help each other. . . . And we could have like counseling and then we could have people like [peer mentor], who was our mentor, we could speak with someone and have them help us. That way we could really . . . That way . . . we were getting into it and not feeling like we were alone or doing this on our own. . . . I was expecting for it just to be a thing where, oh, I know for a fact that I'm going to have some of the same people in my classes, but then it ended up being a thing where it was like we were assigned to groups and we did do a lot of groupwork, and we were able to really get to know each other. And that's how we all became friends, as opposed to my other classes.

Halfway

The instructor spends five minutes going through next week's schedule. A holiday means no class next week. Instead, she would like everyone to go to one of the other sections next week to hear from career services people "to learn about a résumé, to learn how to write a résumé." This goes back and forth between the instructor, students, students, students, instructor, students, students, bouncing around the room, sound bouncing, words in exchange, buzz building, energy ratcheting up. The instructor's voice rises above the buzz: "If you cannot do it for very specific reasons, I can give you another option, but this is our preferred option, for you to come either Wednesday or Thursday. Does everyone understand?" A *yes* buzz flows through the room. "Yes! Great, let's move on!"

Class continues, content continues, side conversations continue. A side conversation is loud enough to make out words, then it lowers to buzz. Then the instructor breaks through to the next topic: "Believe it or not you are halfway done with your first semester of college." At State U., a semester is typically fifteen weeks of instruction plus finals week.

Whats of various inflections fill the room. Some are deadpan statements. Some come with question marks. Some are spoken through looks.

The instructor and the peer mentor simultaneously confirm: "Yes, it's week seven."

Words rise that would haunt a retention specialist: "I've been here too long."

The instructor guides the surprise and disbelief into a plan of action: "Again use next week as a mental break, use next week to check in on your progress in each of your classes."

Teach the Teacher

Learning communities at State U. should have an integrated assignment between at least two of the classes. In planning for imparting this requirement to faculty, there is concern about the faculty response. "I want to make sure that if no one wants to grade the integrated assignment they're not going to say, we're not going to do it," emphasizes the instructor leading this part of the faculty training.

Team grading is an important lesson to impart to people, she continues. "Coming up with a timeline for grading . . ." A fellow facilitator affirms, *they desperately need you for that one.* The instructor agrees. *Right. What does good feedback look like?*

Perhaps a separate webinar could be offered in July to address this topic more thoroughly.

Third Space, Part I

She heard about it all term. Students in one community spend three hours of their Tuesdays and Thursdays in back-to-back classes with each other. And then *class* continued for some of them in the dining hall. It just happened that way, according to one student.

> So, basically, we were just like, we're all hungry. So, we're all just going to migrate to the dining hall and really it really wasn't like a, you know, "Hey, who wants to go," it was sorta kinda like, "Hey, I'm going. Who else wants to tag along?" So, you know, it was really just, you know, are we got one of those, like, I'm not sure if you've been in [dining hall], but one of those huge long tables where we all . . . We took up like one and a half tables, like, most of the class came . . . So, yeah, it was just sorta kinda going in and just, you know, talking about the class, sorta kinda venting about some of the assignments in other classes that weren't necessarily related, you know, asking for help, like, "Oh, how did you guys do X, Y, and Z?" I was like, "Oh yeah, you do it this way."

At points in the term students said the scheduling of their learning community classes back-to-back made the experience feel "like high school."

Going together to a campus dining hall after back-to-back classes was a college twist on this same format.

On occasion, something that happened in the dining hall on Tuesday would show up sideways in class on Thursday, for example, a stepwise increase in social cohesion, or a student in the doghouse with other students. These effects were visible, audible, and palpable but not usually directly attributable to the dining hall, at least by her observation. On occasion, the causal lines were clear, especially to students in these third spaces. One student had a story to share with her about such a moment.

"Okay." He laughs.

> Um, yeah, I dunno. I know that like I personally have a prob-lem with the person with the strong personality type because I enjoyed going [to the dining hall]. So what we would do would, after class we'd always be like, what [major] event is going on, do we want to get food together? And we would all go together. And then the person with the strong personality, the tipping point was a specific thing he had said about me to me, and I was like, this isn't okay. And I was like, I was like, cut it off. I don't want to hang out around you. I don't want to see you. I don't want to be friends with you. I don't want to talk to you. Which meant I had to then . . .

His friend and fellow learning community student jumps in: "Separate, we split off."

"The thing where it's like, 'oh, are we all going to go to the same event together?' did not work anymore. And then I think other people in the, in the community . . . choose to distance or not. I mean like people wanted . . . I don't know if you were there when like he's gotten into spats with other people."

He addresses her directly with this last line. There's been a palpable tension between the students under discussion in her classroom observations, but to this point she wasn't sure why. "I've seen . . . I don't know if I've seen a spat, but I've seen things."

This sparked a similar situation in his mind: "That was priceless between them." A buzz takes over the conversation. He continues to tell about another dining hall incident: "One of the older guys (pause) does not like that kid at all. And they got into a little verbal spat one day, which was really, it was a little funny . . . He's never liked him and they're just one thing. He was just in a bad mood and he just saw the guy do the thing and he's like, okay, I can't handle this anymore. And they had a back and forth."

Here we have third space as a volatile space for forming all types of relationships. She was intrigued, and interjected: "And so is it like these types of moments, like moments outside of class and moments in class or kind of fissures that you can see and kind of like in the way things were—"

His friend brings it full circle. "The social, the social structure? Yeah. Yeah. But yeah, you know, it was an open invite too. So you know, we invited everyone, you know, there's a lot of people, they come most days, so you know, we'd all go into [the dining hall] or something."

The hiding spot for the volatility, the space of possibility for creating and mutating community, reemerges. It's just casual. We all just started going together. Nothing out of the ordinary.

Documenting Effective Educational Practices, Local

This is a vexing question on multiple levels, but she's going to ask it anyway. What's the feature of learning communities you think is most effective for student engagement and/or success? Why?

> I think particularly in the first-year experience . . . it really is having more of those kind of like, like, like I think having the [one-credit learning community class], the like 24-person class can be really helpful. I think the first [three-credit learning community class] has 90 something students in it, which are all learning community students, but the students that aren't in the learning community, they have like a 200-person class. I think . . . they're overwhelmed. They've never been in a, they've never had to think in a room of 200 people before. And so I think, though, like, making it . . .

Pause.

> . . . like I very much tried to be like very real and very personable with my students because like I don't want them to think that like advisors are scary that professors are scary, that people are, are not here to help them. And I mean, not everyone at [State U.] is, but I think a large number of them

more so are, so I think that like having more of a smaller setting, particularly at an institution like [State U.] for all of its characteristics . . . it almost is what makes it sometimes more successful, is probably something that I would say. And also, I think, having like the faculty that talk to each other, like, it's mean but we, like, I found out that someone wasn't attending [the first three-credit learning community class], like, quite frankly, because [the instructor] told me. And so when the student came into my office, I was like, so where are you at on Tuesdays and Thursdays at 8 a.m.? Like what are you doing? So, and I wouldn't have known that."

They both laugh. There seems to be an open line of communication in this community between the instructor of one of the three credit courses and her, the instructor of the one credit major-related course and also an advisor in that major. She can't resist asking about one of the strangest attendance-related things she observed in that three-credit course. It turns into more of a statement than a question.

So, I'm interested in that because as someone who oh my god I never took an 8 AM class to be completely honest in college for good reason. Like it was literally even for me awful to go observe that class at 8 AM all the time. And yeah, I get there, and oh my god until the last week of the term. I swear to you. So, he does attendance by, like, half sheet note cards, right? He cuts them up, he sends them down the aisle. Until the last week of the term I saw students enter the classroom, take out their ID cards and swipe it, in the back on those, those things that are installed in that building. It's just like "he does it manually, you know this." He passes the note cards, why are we still swiping our ID cards? It was bizarre. But it seems like something like attendance. It could be . . . could be, I don't know, let's say, administrator out there who thinks, well, we can just automate that right? If this instructor actually just uses a swipe card machine, then you could see that in EAB [Navigate, a customer relationship management platform], and you wouldn't need to actually talk to a human.

She laughs, maybe nervously. "You could just have data. They could be a red flag for you. So what additionally in talking to [this instructor] helped you out? So, they report attendance and like is there this fuzzy stuff you hear from him, too, this stuff."

"This fuzzy stuff"—an impasse in speech where a concept lives. Is there *more* to producing student engagement through faculty contact than what a vendor product can provide?

Outside In

"The university needs to tell us what's happening in the fall." COVID-19 is wreaking havoc and sowing the seeds of uncertainty among the learning community faculty.

"And they need to introduce us to our teammates in advance," another instructor asserts. "And we need to devote the majority of our workshop time to answering these questions about integrating assignments and getting to know our learning community colleagues."

She asks what else these learning community faculty members would want to change about learning communities on campus. The responses are detailed.

"We just want to know exactly what the learning communities administrators want. We want clear direction on what we're supposed to be doing. What the learning outcomes are."

A voice adds to the kaleidoscope of viewpoints, "During that training yesterday, they asked us "what is integration?" Or something. Why are you asking all these professionals "what is integration?" Are you seriously asking us what integration is? And it was like, once again, you give us all this information that we do not need to know. And the thing we're supposed to be doing, you give us five to ten minutes in the breakout room to do it. What are you doing?"

Another instructor weaves another strand into the fabric of learning community experiences. "We're frustrated with the process." They felt that the central learning community coordinating office should own the learning communities. "So we should be doing very little because it's the [office's] thing. We're just professors. Obviously we'll do the field trips and all that stuff, but the office should take on the brunt of that responsibility."

"And then the other thing is marketing. Prior to COVID, there wasn't any marketing. We didn't know what was happening. And then now we get on meetings with them and it's like . . . there wasn't a whole bunch of forethought about what's happening. It's June!"

Another voice agrees. "Yeah! Like, what else do they do? What else do you do, to where you can't give foresight into what's happening? I can tell you what we do! We get on a call with you and ask ourselves, how can you not have every scenario built out? Like. Don't be taking notes saying that's a good idea. We're on the phone, we should have run through every scenario, because what else do you do?!"

It sounds like the proverbial rocks are being thrown. Just maybe not directly at the learning community administrators.

Caught

Class ends early, but she remains to catch the vibe between classes. She keeps typing, but her notes end abruptly when two students appear right next to her: *So what exactly are you doing back here?*

This is where taking typed notes is a little awkward; she sits there all day and looks at their screens, and now here she is, nervous about people reading hers. Turnabout, fair play, comeuppance, et cetera.

She starts on her usual *student engagement, but not a survey, can see so many more things that don't show up, which is hard, because even then they're not all signals of engagement, like today, the student who was responding to questions asked of the class while his head was still on his desk . . .*

The two students launch from this point into dissing this student. "Yeah, the instructor even opened class yesterday talking through a list of things not to do, and he does all of them." "His feet are always up in his chair." "He sits there on YouTube the whole class."

She notes that the two of them do engagement differently.

One says he prefers lecture format; he learns more when an instructor is speaking to the class like this class is structured. He doesn't need to take notes to remember things, as he isn't that kind of learner. The premade publisher slides work just fine. He discusses the importance of being able to understand what the instructor says. He finds this instructor's speech understandable, even when "a concept that should have four points has 45." A note she believes on the instructor's occasional habit of trailing off into other things.

The other student asks if she sees him playing a game in class: something that's two words, one being "coffee"? She doesn't remember the name; it's unfamiliar to her. She said she has not, but that she does see him take notes, and always in TextEdit. "That's Notepad." Of course! The conversation continues, then Notepad changes its direction:

"B t dubs, fuck this learning community."

Whew, the realness. To be fair, both of them have been keeping it real the whole time. One is sitting directly across the aisle from her in the very back row of the classroom; the other is sitting on the floor in the aisle, a step back from where he sits during class.

Notepad continues. He says the learning community isn't doing anything for him, and the only reason he enrolled in the learning community is to get credits he needs that he lost in transferring to this school. He came with an associate degree, but two classes he earned Cs in didn't transfer, which makes him still a second semester sophomore instead of a junior.

The other student agrees with this sentiment but doesn't restate the exact language. He says the only reason he joined this learning community was to get access to this class: the other sections of it were closed, and he didn't want to have to take philosophy instead. He also wishes his college classes were curved like his high school classes were.

Notepad says he's not sure why college is required for jobs if you know the skills. *I want to get out of here, you want me to get out of here, why are we doing grading like this?* They have a back and forth about the skills you learn from college being obsolete or not after graduation, in the context of coding and software.

Coding languages become obsolete.

No they don't, the most recently developed one was developed twenty years ago.

What about people who learned Microsoft Word 97? They can still use Word today, it's the same structure.

Microsoft Word? He notes he loves the Microsoft server program.

This prompts the other student to start talking about an intro to programming class he's taking this term that he hates; it's too simple. Notepad is a server guy and can't stand coding; he told his advisor, *no coding classes!* The other student gets up to go get his computer from his seat to show Notepad a coding project. Notepad is talking about a coding assignment from his A.A. coursework that was mad long, and there was an error in line three that stopped the whole thing from working.

In this time, the next instructor walks in. A familiar shout of his last name happens at this moment from the class to greet him. She begins to slowly pack up. She puts on her watch, stands up, and puts on her jacket. She wishes the conversation had returned to engagement so she could talk about these ordinary engagements flowing around, but that wasn't to be. This was a delightful substitute. She says her goodbyes: *it's been real*, she says, and gets an "it's been real" back from another student. She notes to the other student in this row that she enjoyed her shimmy when someone's cellphone went off earlier in class. She laughs. She leaves with a peace sign up.

Monolithic Structuring Devices

Student Engagement in higher education is theorized as a significant link between classroom behaviors and measurable student outcomes such as course grades, year-to-year retention, and (on-time) graduation.[2] Engagement is predominately known through measurement, and with the dominance of the NSSE, Engagement data is predominately generated through student self-reports of their Engagement at the conclusion of an experience, a year, or their college career. Engagement, to follow Kuh and colleagues, is a structuring device; it's the link between student input variables and student outcome variables.[3] Engagement is the lever to move a student from where they are when they enter college to where they (or the institution) want them to be when they leave. Engagement produces impact.

Integrative Learning as deployed at State U. is also explicitly a structuring device. Integrative Learning, as specifically evidenced through an assignment shared between the two three-credit classes, is the structure that defines these linked classes as a learning community. Integrative Learning, as defined by the AAC&U, is "an understanding and a disposition that a student builds across the curriculum and co-curriculum, from making simple connections among ideas and experiences to synthesizing and transferring learning to new, complex situations within and beyond the campus."[4] The structure of integrative learning here broadens, though the explicit project here is to render integrative learning through a rubric by which it can be judged evenly across campuses. Integrative learning, in both uses, produces classrooms as high-impact practices.

More Notes on Lecture Format

Lecture format is an expression of the students, faculty, staff, physical spaces, histories, and so on, that come together in the course of a class period. After the fact we can assign agency to particular actors, but the production of lecture format is a bit messier than that. One expression of lecture format came at 8:11 in the morning in late October, right as the instructor was shifting from housekeeping activities that required students to move in ways not typical at the start of this class to housekeeping activities that required students to return to their seats, end interaction with their neighbors, and look to the front: "Phones should be off and away. Everybody in the back who always uses their phones because I can't see them, off and away." This is the protocol to start class. These are words said by the instructor, and only possible within the particular arrangement of class at the time. This type of utterance does not fully shape the class in its image, no matter how much it tries. Usually, it will give form to a class so as to make it recognizable as a lecture. In this instance, it notably doesn't fully shape the class.

Nine minutes later, a Find My iPhone sound goes off loudly in the row behind her.

One minute after this, the default iPhone text message alert sounds in the middle of the same row.

As the classroom clock strikes 8:30 exactly, another iPhone alarm goes off, this time at the front of the room near the lectern. The instructor finally moves to reinforce lecture format: "Y'all, please make sure you have your phones off." The format is in question today.

Fifteen minutes later, yet another alarm goes off. This time, the students are active in the reinforcement of lecture format: a small buzz of student chatter rises from the region of the room where the most recent alarm sounded. Throughout this, the instructor doesn't miss a beat in his response to a student question. Lecture format is an event, a pedagogical circulation of words, sounds, objects, bodies, urgencies, boundaries. It is an event no less powerful than official curriculum review protocols in shaping the structure of this class.

And Now a Word about a Prospective Major Path

"I get plenty of smart students, they have eight calculators on their belts, it's like 'Hey Poindexter,'" he continues in a nasal voice, "'do you want to [help people]?'" They say no, I say out—we need people who want to work with people.

"By the way, I have ten questions. We're on number two. I know if I get close to time, you're going to start packing up. Don't!" He pauses a beat. You'll never be a [profession from this major]."

"Don't do or not do this program because I'm funny, or not." This is a tough field, and you won't be able to work while you're in school. "It's hard, it's really hard."

"If I see a spelling error . . . phew!" He makes a tossing motion with his arm, as if tossing a student's major application away. "I throw it away! I don't give it the time of day! That [is a crucial] mistake . . . have an alternate plan, what do they call it? Have parallel plans if you don't get into the program you want."

"The reason why I have 10 to 12 students is so that they can spell out [major nickname at graduation] . . . no it's only because I have 10 to 12 [field placements]. The reason I'm here, I don't need students, I have all the students I need, but in case you're interested . . ."

He cracks jokes to lighten things up, but it's clear—he said it exactly—he does not need these students in his major, he is here talking to them as a courtesy in case anyone would like to compete to be in his major. It is an interesting take on the major pitch. It is singular. It is not a pitch at all. It is not someone clamoring for enrollment or hard selling experiences.

Performance Expectations Set at Appropriately High Levels

A topic in today's class is race and ethnicity, and specifically prejudice and discrimination. In this class, the instructor involves students in class usually to respond to quick probes he intersperses throughout the lecture. He asks questions that can be answered quickly, gets several responses, and then moves back to lecturing from slides. The performance expectations of students during class, beyond the rote "no laptops no phones" rule, and likely some expectations about taking notes and not sleeping, are implicitly to participate every once in a while to make this structure work. Today's student contributions to classroom discussion exceed this implicit expectation.

She notes the topic and the room composition. There are about ninety students registered for the class, though it doesn't feel like the room is totally full today. The class appears to have large numbers of both Black and white students in it, with far smaller numbers of Latinx and Asian students. The instructor has already identified himself to the class as part Asian. He did this earlier today, but he quite memorably also did this weeks ago: "I'm part Asian, but that doesn't mean I was born knowing how to use chopsticks." His reminder today comes as he reviews a slide on the social construction of race and asks the class *what racial characteristics we attribute to Asian folks.* Of the types of questions he usually asks of students, this seems likely to stir something up. It's unclear what. She gets an uneasy feeling that's mixed with anticipation. Where in the world is he going to take this? Her notes circle in this impasse from direct student quotes to directly quoting the slides to noting environmental shifts in the room. It's in this context that the instructor launches one of his most audacious questions to the class so far this term:

What are some prejudices about white people?

A white student quickly jumps in: "That we're all privileged."

The buzz in the room ignites. It is loud and immediate. A Black student with their head on their desk makes eye contact with her and rolls his eyes. This appears to be a buzz of vehement disagreement. The instructor tries to bring the class back to lecture format:

"We're going to come back to that one, if not now, Thursday, let's not go with that one, let's not go with that one. Being white in America, it may not be like being a millionaire, but being white in America, it comes with a certain level of privilege."

And with this experience of how his last question landed, he continues: "Okay, Black people."

The class does not bite. They experienced his last question too. There's a pause that follows his statement and a feeling on her part that since his last question didn't go well, students are waiting to see who is going to jump in. The instructor finally fills the gap. He tells the class that there is a prejudice that Black people commit more crime. He now asks the class to name racial stereotypes again: "Asian people."

A student speaks up to say Asian people eat rice with everything.

"Black people."

A white student speaks up to say, "Black people are naturally good at sports," and a Black student immediately adds "Black people love fried chicken and watermelon."

She still has this uneasy feeling mixed with anticipation. "White people."

Perhaps this is what all of this has been building toward. Or not. A Black student quickly jumps in to offer "white people don't season their food." The class falls out with buzz, and more than buzz: noticeable laughter. The lid has come off. The stereotypes keep coming: "white people can't dance," "white people can't jump." A Black student behind her adds that "in situations of danger, white people are gullible." The buzz stays strong in this section with this one. A buzz of agreement? A geography of buzz marked by racial segregation in classroom seating?

The instructor brings this section of class to a close. "Why haven't I said 'Mexican' or 'Latino'?" Students correctly note that Mexican and Latino are not races, but in the words of the instructor, they are nationalities that comprise multiple races.

The buzz has died off and student performance recedes to the usual expected level. The instructor explains a stereotype about Mexicans being lazy that no one in the class indicated they were familiar with before. Was this a high level of expectation to begin with?

Noise

1. Class starts, and students are still chatting with each other. The instructor calls out, "If we could suspend the chatter now and move on."

2. A student in the back of the room rather noisily stands up and moves seats so she can plug in her laptop.

3. A student arrives late and noisily sits down. The instructor reacts. "If you do need to be late, let's try to come in quietly."

4. Someone's keys drop to the floor.

5. A student in the back of the room ratchets the blinds to block out the sun.

6. One student in the back of the room constantly sniffles, as if needing to blow her nose.

7. A student sneezes. Another says, "bless you."

8. A metal water bottle topples over and clanks on the floor.

9. The students next to her are whispering to each other. About what, she isn't sure.

10. Students start stuffing laptops into backpacks while the instructor is still teaching.

Meerkats

The out-of-class excursion to the zoo continues.[5] She catches up with the class that's waiting in front of another exhibit. The ground in the massive cage is rocky and sandy. Meerkats are peeking out of holes in the ground.

The instructor asks, *What is the theory that applies to this situation?* A student replies with a guess. The instructor affirms it's a good guess.

One of the students is on a phone call. "Mom, I'm at the zoo . . . this is class, I guess. Ok bye. She said, 'this is what I'm paying for?'"

The group moves on to the next exhibit.

Meerkats are posing for pictures.

A Conversation about Inequality

A student rests his head in his hands. His eyes are closed. Music starts playing on the other side of the wall. The noise seems to stir no reaction in the students or instructor.

"What are some prestigious jobs?" the instructor asks. Pens go down. This part must not be important according to whatever criteria students use to measure importance.

"Lawyer," one student responds. "CEO," another murmurs. "Everything your mom wants you to be!" a third chimes in. The instructor chuckles in response.

"What about low prestige?" he goes on. The students' answers include garbage people, waiters, janitors.

Think about if there weren't trash collectors . . . in our city, you get one bin, and I'm single . . . I recently managed to destroy yet another relationship, so I'm single . . .

Reluctant chuckles and murmurs flit across the room. There is a sense of awkwardness and TMI, but maybe this doesn't matter. It certainly doesn't seem to matter to the instructor.

"I'm single, and I still manage to fill up that bin, and the person who picks up the trash makes more than I do."

The instructor moves on to another theory, and about half the class starts writing again. A few students watch the instructor pace back and forth, while others are looking at the screens in the front of the class.

According to this theory, the instructor intones, you would be more engaged if you think this subject is important to your major; you would take more notes, talk more—each class is different because of the individuals that are in it. Oh crap, we've run out of time. Next time have chapter 2 read.

Class concludes abruptly. Out come the cellphones, and several students start talking to each other. One student goes to the instructor's desk with his laptop to get help with accessing the textbook. The instructor addresses the class, reiterating that students can reach him on his cell phone with course-related questions.

She wonders how many of these students will take the instructor up on his offer.

Coordination

Looking back at the term, what was the most difficult aspect of it as it relates to student learning or engagement?

> Unfortunately I wasn't able to coordinate with the other professors in our group because we weren't supposed to have come together to design, you know, one or two assignments that the students would participate in. We weren't able to do that. So we were all sort of like going solo. I'm talking about the professors; we were all going solo. In fact, had we had the meeting in May of this year, we would have done better with, you know, combining resources to, to have a better experience for the students in the fall. But it looks like that meeting is gonna be online. It's going to be via Zoom, like, you know, like I'm meeting with you right now via Zoom. So I think the fact that we weren't able to coordinate activities or, or at least one major activity, I think that took away from the goal of the [learning communities program] itself. You know. I felt like I wasn't able to get my students to fully benefit from the [learning community] because I wasn't able to coordinate with the other two instructors to come up with a common assignment for them. Maybe a trip to . . . Because I know that the previous year, if I'm correct, they made a trip to [location] to

a [field-of-study-related location], or some place in [the city], they went somewhere . . .

Redirect

So, you don't like your other learning community teacher. Evidently, the instructor has picked up on the students' grumbling over the past two weeks. It doesn't take long for students to open up and share their impressions of their other instructor. The atmosphere in the room is a mix between agitation and resignation.

"So, what should they do?" the instructor asks the peer mentor. Multiple students continue their lament. "She's grouchy!" one complains. "Or she'll say something to make us all feel dumb!" adds another. *And our test is on Monday*, a third explains.

"How do you feel about the test?" The instructor tries to bring class back to academic matters. The peer mentor finally gets a chance to speak. *This is a great learning experience about how to deal with a bad professor. Especially since you can't drop the class.* Inwardly, she cringes. Not sure the learning community administrators would want their peer mentors labeling learning community faculty as "bad." Or any faculty for that matter.

"Y'all gotta get through it." The instructor encourages the students to be persistent. A quiet voice insists, "We're not trying to be disrespectful; we're just trying to help our peers and it makes her upset." In response, the instructor makes his final point. "Since you all know this, let's have these conversations after class, just to shift some of the tension in the class."

Words of wisdom. Two weeks down, fourteen weeks to go.

What Does Buzz Do?

Buzz as an observed and felt affect in these learning communities is in its first instance a sonic experience. Buzz is a sonic field whose constituent words are indiscernible. It's the sound of words without their content. It's the sound of something happening. It's the sound of being moved by the classroom experience.

Buzz, a primarily but not exclusively sonic experience, carries attendant embodiments. First of these is the presumed still and silent state of all persons but one in a space that allows buzz to become tangible. This stillness and silence were often experienced by students in this learning community as engagement. Stillness and silence can slip into checking phones, taking a cat nap, or other disengagements. Engagement as used here is fuzzy. Stillness and silence, or other perceptible, observable, and measurable ways of being in class, are imperfect. Affect comes before these. Buzz, as one affect, is the sound of being moved by the classroom experience that is prior to our ability to classify such movement as engagement or disengagement. We expect some of you will be moved to embody the characteristics of what we otherwise classify as engaged and disengaged students. Some of you will be moved to embody buzz itself—by producing a sonic or visual buzz of your own—mediated as it is for us as a collective by this page.

New Contributors

Today's topic of discussion is education. The instructor informs the class that the proportion of people with high school diplomas increased from 25 percent to 88 percent from 1940 to 2014. His glass this morning is half empty. *But that also means that 12 percent of 350 million people don't even have a high school education.*

Most students are leaned back in their chairs. She sees two coffee cups, one from the local coffee shop and one from Starbucks. She also notices three plastic water bottles and a coffee drink in a glass bottle. A student raises his hand and says that 12 percent of 350 million is 42 million. Forty-two million people without a high school diploma in the United States.

The next student raises his hand and asks, "Couldn't you argue that you don't want everyone to go to college?" The instructor exclaims, "There you go!" He grins and points his finger at the student who asked the question. "You're looking at it from a [theory] point of view."

The lecture continues until the instructor asks, "Are students acting the way you would expect?" A cellphone ringer goes off, causing the instructor to laugh. "I couldn't have planned that any better."

At 10:09 a.m., a student in the back row checks the time on her phone. Her facial expression is neutral, though perhaps she was hoping they'd be further along. Or perhaps she is waiting for a text from a friend. Another student answers the instructor's question about why they wouldn't want everyone having a college degree because of the need for low-level labor. Yet another student asks about folks not going to school in the 1940s but still making good money without a college degree. "Wouldn't that be [this theory]?" she asks.

This is the most talkative the class has been all term. It's still incredibly quiet as students copy down notes from the screen, but two students who have rarely if ever contributed to class did so verbally today.

Waiting for a Moment

Students are waiting outside a classroom on the second floor of the humanities building. She can hear them from three hallways away as soon as she gets out of the stairwell. The students are speaking animatedly with each other, apparently unaware of their surroundings outside of faculty offices. Thankfully, faculty office doors are closed. There is a familiarity and great excitement about today's class. Students shush each other as the noise level ratchets up. It helps subdue the buzz temporarily. Then it spirals upward again. More shushing.

This boisterous level of conversation is in stark contrast to their first day of class, and maybe that's expected in a hallway. Maybe these students will form a community in spite of the challenges the atmosphere in one of their learning community classes brings to the party. The very thought of sitting in front of an instructor in a contentious classroom environment brings chills down her spine. If there is a sense of community, then does that equal Engagement? Does it meet the goals of university administration?

The instructor arrives and explains he is waiting on their guest speaker for the day. Students whisper to each other. She is unable to make out what they are saying. The chatter gets really loud (again) and one of the students shushes the group. She is concerned they are disturbing someone's work. Most of the students appear not to share her concern and continue to chatter. It's like an orchestra warming up on the big stage ahead of a symphonic performance. Mahler 2 comes to mind, as if one were a choir member sitting patiently in the chairs behind the brass waiting to hear the tuning to Concert A.

She is sitting with the peer mentor on a bench in the hallway. As the group is waiting, a student walks over to the pair and asks the peer mentor how long he studied for his graduate school admissions exam. He explains his process to the student. The student listens intently, nodding at his advice. There is a myriad of side conversations as the instructor discusses the benefits of taking an introductory science course should students score poorly on their placement tests. A student murmurs, "Yeah, it's looking real intro-ish for me . . ." She suppresses a chuckle.

The instructor checks his phone one last time for a message from their guest speaker. Still nothing. Eventually, he dismisses class and the students leave, including a large group that departs via an enormous elevator. The elevator doors close slowly.

There. Silence. Finally, the Concert A.

What's in a Name?

Two months prior to the start of the semester, there are still instructors who don't know the name of their learning community. One of the administrators explains that faculty were informed of this along with the hiring of their peer mentors. Another emphasizes the need to streamline communication. The first rolls her eyes. "Homeslice, what do you want me to do?!"

One instructor has asked to change the name of their learning community. Staff discuss the feasibility of this for a moment, then realize that promotional materials have already been sent to print.

It's just too late.

Another administrator points out: *If I were faculty, and you told me I couldn't change the name of my class, I'd be pretty upset, too.*

Colorful

Later that same week in another learning community, the instructor delivers the same lecture.

"What are some prejudices about white people?" A student responds, "They're prejudiced!"

"What about Black people?" the instructor continues. "They're loud," comes a reply.

Moving the conversation on to stereotypes, the instructor explains that they are more specific than prejudice. "What is a stereotype about Asians? Not only are they smart they are . . . ?" A student wagers a guess. "Good at math."

Seemingly out of nowhere, a student exclaims, "Watermelon and fried chicken!" The instructor asks, "Who?" "Black people!" the student responds. Two Black women have a different opinion. "I don't even like watermelon," says one. "Watermelon is nasty!" agrees the other.

The class moves on from food to crime. Black people are more likely to become criminals. White people are more likely to do hard drugs.

Animated discussion ensues.

Public Demonstration of Competence

Another day of final presentations. Another day of higher-than-usual (of late) class attendance. It's fascinating to watch each group adopt in their own way the mannerisms of the instructor when they present. She isn't even sure if they are always mannerisms of this instructor—perhaps mannerisms of a composite instructor, an image of an instructor. She arrived at class two minutes late today and already managed to miss the first group presentation of the day. She settles in for the second presentation in the seat usually occupied by the peer mentor. The peer mentor isn't here today. Her two tablemates and her note to each other that we can't remember the last time all three of us were in this class together. She says it's been at least a month. The collective isn't sure that it's been only a month.

The second group begins with a call to order that she hasn't heard in this class all term, from the instructor or anybody else: "If you have a laptop or phone out, please put them away, we are about to present, and we want your attention . . . I will ask you to leave." As she said in her field notes—well damn! Demonstrating competence is not just demonstrating knowledge but demonstrating the mannerisms of those the institution deems as knowledge-keepers. The mannerisms of this class's knowledge keeper of late has been to show videos for at least half of the class. This group, much like the others who have presented so far, begins with a video. She continues taking field notes through this time, and as she types away on her laptop, the student next to her leans over with a smile to ask if she got the no laptop memo. She tries to laugh without making the sound of laughter. She should have put her laptop away, but she continues to type.

The video ends. Others should have put their phones away too but didn't. One person seems authorized to have their phone out: they are taking pictures of the group presenting. Other students are just very obviously staring at their laps or their desks. These slides look put together. The presentation has lasted far longer than others, and it doesn't show signs of slowing down yet. Is this competence? Another group member comes up to present, the slide changes, and the aesthetic shifts: where the previous slides looked pulled together, this displays a pixelated Venn diagram. Even with the length of this presentation, there are still no heads on desks. Is that Engagement? The presentation ends after thirteen minutes. The group gives a standard-fare closing to presentations in this class: "That's it, thanks very much, if you have any questions feel free to ask after class." To end a public demonstration of competence in this class—by practice, not by rule—is to not drag things out with questions.

Before the group members can walk back to their seats, however, they are stopped by a student with a question. The student wants the presenters to go back a few slides. The presenter of the Venn diagram slide asks, somewhat self-deprecatingly, "You mean to the blurry one?" Nope, another one before that. The student and then the instructor engage in a back-and-forth discussion with multiple presenters. This isn't the world the presenters likely had in mind when ending their presentation. Or maybe it is, and they were trying to speak another one into existence. The first presenter tries to end things with a quick "any other questions? No? Thanks very much." This too does not work. Now a student has a question about the blurry slide. Three minutes into a question-and-answer time that has been standard in these presentations, and that every single group has tried to wiggle out of, the group once again attempts to speak their desires into being: "Okay thank you guys." A buzz arises from the class—it seems to be a cheerbuzz. There is one word audible: yay! The presenters now have coconspirators in their attempts to finish. The instructor has another question—will this presentation continue? The instructor appends six crucial words to the end of their question: "You guys can take a seat." It's over. The group sits down. What started as a question to the group becomes a class discussion of a usual sort, one taken over by someone who takes over conversations.

A thirteen-minute presentation. Three minutes of questions. All group members participated in the sharing of information with the class. Two minutes of video shown. Zero heads on desks. One laptop out. An unknown number of phones in use.

Striving toward the Pinnacle

As it turns out, faculty can have an entire conversation about course integration in metaphors and similes.

"Integration is a zipper."

"Exactly. It's like interlacing your fingers."

"In fact, integration is somewhat like a quiche. I wouldn't eat an onion by itself. I wouldn't eat a mushroom by itself. But when you put all the ingredients together it's something different. It's delicious."

———

As it turns out, administrators can have an entire conversation about training faculty in metaphors and similes.

"We're clearly the wranglers next week."

"Exactly. They want to know when they can expect enrollment numbers for fall. This is not any different than any other year. It's not a question where I can look in a crystal ball and tell you."

"I agree. Thank you for handling that train that was going off the rails for a minute."

Another staff member chimes in. "I know she thinks I'm going to wave my wand and everything is done digitally."

"She doesn't recognize we're constrained by red tape."

"This song and dance went well though."

"Yes. We've got them on the path, and now we need to move them along the path."

"Speaking of that, what fat can be trimmed from Day 2 of the workshop?"

She answers her own question. "We could offer follow-up sessions on low-hanging fruit throughout the summer."

———

As it turns out, you can have an entire conversation about planning for Engagement in metaphors and similes.

Alignment

We meet weekly to debrief the week's notes. Is anything noteworthy? Everything is noteworthy. Everything is anecdote. Our goal here is to paint as complete a picture as possible, knowing that complete is a fiction and that everything is not knowable. Nevertheless, we try to jot down as much of what we experience as possible. ABT. Always be typing.

An example: For one learning community class, one of our field note entries numbers 279 words for the first day of observation. The same author noted 1,253 words on the last day of that same class. Most notes were captured with word processing software while some were handwritten, especially in the beginning.

But what matters isn't the number of words but rather their level of detail. Detail is where anecdote lives; it's the location of the sights and sounds and affects that comprise the composition of learning communities and student engagement at State U. Sometimes anecdotes are clarified by ABT, and sometimes anecdotes are clarified by sitting back and attuning to a particular moment in class. These details, big and small, are entanglements[6] with an ordinary world, a world that refuses to be captured in its entirety.

Defiance

She arrives to class early. Four students are in the room sitting quietly, others are slowly trickling in. Everyone is on their cell phone or laptop. The instructor is sitting behind the desk at the front of the room. She attempts to make conversation with the students, asking them if they are taking an English class this term. Several students affirm. A police siren goes off outside. It's a startling noise in an otherwise quiet classroom. A student walks in, talking softly on her phone, and takes a seat in the back row. The three students next to her start talking to each other under their breath. The rest of the room is still quiet.

Class starts when the instructor closes the door to lock the room. Out of 23 registered students in the class, 14 are currently present. Several students have open laptops on their desks. One of them is following along with the PowerPoint on her screen. The others are not. The student next to her is rapidly scrolling through Instagram on her phone.

9:04 a.m. A knock on the door. Two students come in late. This isn't the first time these particular two have arrived late.

9:06 a.m. Another late arrival.

9:07 a.m. Another late arrival, another repeat offender.

The instructor poses questions, and several students offer answers that appear to be not quite on target. Their answers are shot down by the instructor. A girl in the front of the room grins and shakes her head. She is on her phone. She mouths something to someone across the room before going back to her phone to text someone. Maybe someone in the class. She huffs and props a sweater under her head before leaning her head against the wall.

There is more active texting, now from at least six students. No one is taking notes. There are no notebooks on top of desks. There is music from headphones from a student in the back row. Another student yawns loudly. The instructor asks another question, and a student raises his hand. The instructor doesn't acknowledge him, so he lowers his hand. Two students chuckle at this. Another loud yawn. Two students have their heads on their desks.

The fifty-minute class ends after forty minutes. She breathes a sigh of relief.

Peer Mentor Time

The next presenter will be here soon. Let's hear a bit from the peer mentor before then. The peer mentor, summoned by the instructor, walks to the front of the room.

There's an event on Thursday, check the group chat.

A lot of folks "have asked me, 'What happens if I test out of a course and it won't let me register?'" He gives an example of a science class restriction. "An easy way to get out of this is to call the registrar's office . . . if they're like I can't really help you with that, then you contact the professor themselves, you say 'Hey, my name is [name], I'm a freshman in the History department, and . . .'" The example continues.

"Oh what else. I turn twenty-two on Thursday, so I got that going on." The class erupts in low cheers and clapping. Celebrationbuzz.

The next speaker walks in, and the peer mentor goes back to his seat.

Faculty Connections

Class moves on, and one student is tapping on the enclosure's glass to get a lion's attention. In the next exhibit, it smells strongly like animals. There are two adult giraffes and a youth inside their house, and the keepers are working to let them out. One student comments on how nasty the poop is in the enclosure.

Trailing behind the group, one student takes pictures of the ostrich, "I feel like I'm the only one actually excited." She replies, "Super geeking out?" The student exclaims, "Yeah!" She responds saying, "I get that."

Most of the students stick with each other while walking, but three of them are talking with one of the instructors while moving through the zoo. "I can't swim, and the Air Force is too hard to get into." Another student exclaims, "I like when you teach. You're the only class I really like. We get upset when you're not there."

They move out of earshot, so she fails to hear the instructor's response.

Third Space, Part II

What programmatic opportunities were provided to facilitate student community outside of class?

> Really it was the [one credit learning community] class, we had a group project that I thought, you know, really forced us to work together and just sorta kinda more of the this, you know, it was the group projects in some of the classes, you know, we got together in small groups, the groups weren't the same each time. We sorta kinda got together, worked together. You know, we chatted in the GroupMe. I don't know if you've seen the WeChat chatting groups like that and stuff just, you know, connect outside of class and stuff like that. It was really it was really just sorta kinda, it was sorta kinda like I wanna say, like, you know, forced, but we were just kind of like, thrown together at one point, and they're just kind of like, you know, you know, it's sorta kinda you just have to jump right into it. Just to get it to be effective. So, you're just sorta kinda jumping right into that.

Groupwork

A student walks into the classroom and loudly exclaims, *There she is!* Suddenly, several students turn toward her and ask whether she attended their morning class. She hadn't been able to. There was a multicar accident on the highway, and she got held up in the stopped traffic.

Sparks erupt at various seats throughout the room as the students share what happened in their other learning community class that morning. Animatedly, one student says, "Our professor was late, too." Another agrees, "Yeah, I got held up too." Voices get louder as more students join the conversation. "She was mean!" She had us help pick each other topics for a narrative essay . . . Incensed, a student calls out ". . . and then she said, 'are you listening?' "—"Stop your extracurricular conversations." Students are gathered near her seat, expressing their frustration. "She said 'let's talk about this' and then when we were talking as a group she got mean." Students talk across one another, and it's difficult to catch everyone's voice. "And she said Friday we'll have a pop quiz and when we asked on what she said, 'read the syllabus.' "

During this time, several students on the other side of the room turn around and ask where she was that morning. Meanwhile, the instructor has walked into the classroom, and the attendance sheet is being passed around from student to student to be signed. The sparks of dissatisfaction are beginning to dim. The noise level simmers down as the instructor starts class. To be continued another time, to be sure.

Toward a Definition

We do not enter the field as blank slates. Dozens of researchers have published results of studies concerning learning communities. They read that learning community students made academic achievements beyond those of their non-learning community peers.[7] They read that some outcomes regarding learning community participation aren't altogether favorable.[8] And they read, perhaps most intriguingly, that learning community students become more Engaged throughout their participation.[9]

Engagement, the word itself, seems both straightforward and all-encompassing and at the same time is nevertheless elusive in its definition. Is Engagement a greater sense of peer belonging or a collaborative approach to learning?[10] Is it indicated by students making greater academic efforts on their educational journeys or simply a greater satisfaction with their college experience overall?[11] Or is Engagement exemplified by a greater quality of learning than that experienced by non-learning community students?[12] Is it marked by time on task or quality of time?[13]

As time continued, we began to ask similar questions of integrative learning. Questions upon questions in "a space of time lived without a narrative genre."[14]

What exactly are they looking for in their observations? And perhaps more importantly, how would they represent any of these indicators?

Space

The room is about one-third too large for the class. There is a lot of space in between clusters of students. There is a lot of distance between the instructor in the front and the back row. But no one sits in the back back row.

Making Connections

The instructor stands on a wooden bench across the paved path in front of the bald eagle exhibit. The students are crowded in clumps in front of the bench. Two students have ear buds in their ears but in general students appear to be listening.

"Who is Casper Schmidt?" asks the instructor. That's the name engraved on a plaque on the bench on which he is standing. One student replies that Schmidt is likely a philanthropist from the local area. The instructor goes on to lecture about commemorating people. *How much do you think it would cost to donate a bench when a brick is $100? It's probably $1,500 to get a bench.* "From a [theory] point of view, not everyone can afford that." She is surprised that this out-of-class enrichment activity is being used as an opportunity to reinforce class material.

Pointing to the eagle perched in the exhibit behind the students, the instructor mentions that the eagle is the nation's bird. *And eagles mate for life,* he says. *Monogamy and faithfulness were referenced in chapter 3.*

Class moves along toward the oyster pond. Three students are on their phones texting or scrolling. One student is taking a selfie with two other students. The pond smells.

Zooming Along

The meeting host gets up and leaves the screen, presumably tending to something in her home. A few minutes later, all of the participants are all booted from the Zoom meeting because someone else started the same meeting as the host. None of them knew this was possible. They return to the meeting and settle in, maybe for the long haul this time.

Throughout the meeting, the majority of attendees are muted. Several of them also have their cameras turned off.

The supervisor starts the meeting by welcoming those in attendance. There is audio feedback. She interrupts herself and asks "is someone talking? Did someone ask a question?" The meeting host asks folks to mute themselves. One instructor mumbles to themselves, "mute yourself . . . how do you do that?"

Twenty-five minutes into the meeting, there is active silence as faculty work, reflecting on an assignment. At this point, about a dozen or so have their cameras turned off. Two faculty are called on to share their thoughts with the groups. One turns on his camera before he responds. The other does not.

A third instructor leaves his seat in front of the computer. His screen is empty but for half of a tan couch and a front door.

A facilitator screen shares AAC&U's integrative learning rubric of high-impact practices with the group.

More than half of the cameras are now turned off.

The next facilitator shares her screen. The document reads "Learning Communities: Fall 2020 'Big Questions'"

The graduate assistant reposts the agenda link in the chat. They are forty-eight minutes into the workshop. Four of the faculty have their head resting on a hand, with their elbows propped on their desks.

Despite having prepopulated breakout rooms ahead of the meeting, about fifteen faculty don't automatically get assigned into their groups. The host works manually for approximately nine minutes to assign the remaining faculty to their rooms.

Like whack-a-moles, folks keep popping back into the main meeting room with questions about whether or not they got sent to the appropriate room. One of them jokes, "Nobody wants me." He remains in the main room and works on the assignment solo.

At some point, the supervisor rejoins the call, apparently having signed off earlier. She immediately mutes herself and turns off video.

A few minutes later, the host closes the breakout rooms and little by little the faculty return to the main screen.

"Well this is so embarrassing, I just noticed my bed isn't made up in the background," exclaims the supervisor. A few folks chuckle in response.

Finally, everyone is back and unlike before, most cameras are now turned on. The host explains that attendees are welcome to unmute themselves to ask questions and ends the meeting.

Several folks unmute themselves to say thank you. A few wave their hands goodbye.

Once all of the faculty are gone, the administrators begin to debrief the workshop. The graduate assistant turns on her camera and asks the host to end the recording before answering a controversial question that was posed by the group.

Follow Up

It's been four months since the student was enrolled in his learning community. She meets with him in Zoomland, the alternative to in-person interactions during a now-raging pandemic. What remains for this student from the carefully crafted communities, implemented with intentionality? This student is enthusiastic.

> I still feel that the experience really helped the transition to college. And just so we're kind of build a social structure that I was kinda and just taking you back to sorta pandemic thing are kind of I was relying on I made a lot of new friends and met a lot of new people inside of the learning community that, you know, I still hung out with and, you know, did stuff outside. And there was just a lot of, I was really nervous about college and just having sorta a set support structure. I was . . . it, it made me feel really good to have that.

He punctuates his reminiscing by smiling at the screen.

They chat about student organizations, major-related activities, classroom spaces. The conversation goes from résumé development during the first year in college to awkward instructors to the peer mentor who was good when she was there. But he was unable to attend any of the peer mentor-coordinated activities.

"I think the most meaningful experience, honestly," the student continues,

> I still do have to say it's just the community that was built, you know. We had three classes together, we got to know each other, you know, our classes were engaging. I felt that in those

classes, we were able to just, you know, we're more comfortable with each other, you know, we're more comfortable to answer questions, more comfortable to interact with the professors, you know, since we were all in there together and we all knew we all knew everyone from the start. There was just, it was just a lot easier just to just to kinda speak up in the class and just, you know, ask for help because we had that, you know, set community. We weren't just me for an hour, two or three times a week. We were together for at least, was it two . . . five hours a week at least we were together.

The conversation is comfortable now. The student shares about coursework connections and transferring in credits and starting master's level coursework as a second-year student. In the learning community, he notes, *they were forced to work together in groups, which was hard for someone who is not outgoing. The students chatted using GroupMe, which helped.*

They continue their conversation about making connections. Joining campus organizations. Finding community.

In Between

Idle chitchat between staff members turns substantive. *Is everything okay given that you've been pulled into lots of meetings with our supervisor lately?* One of the learning community administrators responds with "Registration woes." Apparently, the office is in the middle of reviewing what the registration process for learning communities is going to look like. Another administrator smirks. *It's a matter of trying our new process and seeing what fails.*

The process is thus: Students fill out an interest form, staff use the interest forms to register them. *Are you able to accept the block?* The learning community coordinator replies, "No, and we have to send information to the advisors to make sure they don't register them for other classes."

Just then, her printer finally turns back on and starts printing documents. "I was able to get a little bit of ink from our supervisor but now we have no budget."

The Digital Order of Things

On[15] Zoom
May 29: Planning Meeting for Day 1
June 2: Faculty Workshop Day 1
June 2: Workshop Day 1 Debrief Meeting
June 3: Planning Meeting for Day 2
June 5: Second Planning Meeting for Day 2
June 9: Faculty Workshop Day 2
June 9: Workshop Day 2 Debrief Meeting

———

Via Email
June 25: IMPORTANT UPDATE: Cancellation of Fall 2020 Learning Communities

Chapter Three

Difference (2020–21)

Zoom Tile Life

Last year, classroom life in learning communities consisted of lectures in physical classrooms. We had conversations in hallways before and after classes, and we attended trainings and other meetings in physical meeting spaces. This year, each of us sit at our internet home. For most of us, this is at our place of residence, be it a dorm room or off-campus dwelling. For some students, this is in the campus library, using computers in tenuous proximity with those presumably outside of their pandemic bubble in this prevaccine world. We come together through the medium of Zoom videoconferencing, a relatively unknown platform to many at the beginning of the pandemic. We join classrooms and meetings in our (quasi-) individual tiles, sometimes with others in camera view, often muted for much of a session. We may have our cameras turned on, or off, and we may be dressed in clothes we would otherwise wear if we were meeting in person, dressed as we would otherwise only from the waist up, and in the case of some students, not dressed at all. Most of us are on camera unmasked, but those joining from public campus spaces wear masks, providing some protection from their surroundings while obscuring half of their face from view. Lectures become screen shares where the instructor can't easily see students who are now rendered tile by tile in the Zoom user interface. Conversations before and after class may become emails, text messaging exchanges, or may not happen at all. Even meetings among State U. administrators are reduced to conversations between Zoom tiles with variously muted microphones and turned-off cameras. In these meetings, participants may actively be working on course prep or responding to emails, but that isn't necessarily new with pandemic life, rather differently facilitated by this particular socio-technical climate.

The educational world as we knew it is changed. For those familiar with learning community classroom life at State U. before now, these classroom practices are familiar and strange at once. For students new to State U. and to higher education, the comparison of familiar and strange can't be based on prior personal experiences but rather on expectations. With all the talk of our collective disruption, unprecedented times, and the development of a new normal, it would seem that the practices of classroom life are quite strange in comparison to expectations. This year feels different than last year; it *is* different. In what ways is this drumbeat of conversations about a new normal tied to practices or to anticipations? Is our attachment to re/definitions of a new normal instead—or also—a cruel optimism, an attachment to an object that impedes our progress toward returning to the classroom practices we miss? Is the new normal a structuring device that categorizes our anecdotes as impasses forged by crisis that must be resolved through reengagement, reintegration, and increased impact rather than creating value anew in practices of critical anticipation?[1]

Muted Classroom Life

Chat is enabled today. Forty-four minutes into class and nothing has been written in the chat at all.

She is observing three students in their individual Zoom tiles. Their cameras are on, and their microphones are muted. The student on the left is propped up in the corner of her bed, leaning against two white cinder block walls. The room is lit by an overhead light. The student is looking off screen and huddled in a comforter.

The instructor introduces the video referenced as the "Harlow experiment" in the textbook and plays the clip. It's this horrific documentary of an inhumane experiment on infant monkeys. She remembers the clip from the year before and mutes the sound on her laptop so as not to hear the infant monkey's cries for its mother.

As the clip ends, she focuses again on the three tiles of students. One of them appears to have fallen asleep. To her surprise, there appears to be no verbal response to the video clip from students, and there is no written reaction in the chat. Perhaps students haven't realized it's back enabled. Perhaps the clip didn't spark any outrage or dismay in them. Perhaps they, too, had their sound muted and are sitting in front of their cameras to receive credit for attending without actually attending. Perhaps their feelings are as muted as their microphones.

(Une Pièce de) Resistance

Via email: Faculty make it clear they'll be attending the summer workshops because they are a prerequisite for receiving their learning community stipends. They're busy. Or maybe they don't need workshopping. Other faculty let the central learning community coordinating office know they still don't know who their faculty partners are. They haven't received any communication. Should they still attend? Yet another faculty member writes: "Well, I'm not going to have my stuff ready."

In breakout rooms: Faculty are asked to collaborate on integrative learning pieces for their learning community. One facilitator is informed that this particular group of learning community faculty has been teaching this learning community for a minute. To be asked to design (or even fine tune) integrated assignments and joint syllabi statements seems superfluous. "There's still room to grow," the facilitator laments after the workshop. In another breakout room, this one without a facilitator, the faculty's conversation drifts to forced online learning and lack of contact with students. The female faculty member is muted. The men are talking among themselves, one exclaiming: "in-person classes . . . that's what college should be."

In evaluations: Given the opportunity to share feedback about the first part of the workshop, faculty have questions. *The university needs to tell us what's happening in the fall. When can we expect enrollment numbers? How can I change the name of my learning community?*

Craft Time

There is another guest speaker leading the class today. There have been a wide variety of different campus resources presented to students over the last several weeks. As the guest speaker talks with the students about the importance of volunteerism, a student captures her attention. What is she doing? The student appears to be knitting or crocheting; although she can't be sure which it is. She can see the movement of the student's arms and a piece of white yarn around her left fingers. The student is looking down and unravels a length of yarn from a white ball. This is unexpected and intriguing to her. As the class session continues, she periodically focuses on the student, attempting to ascertain if the activity is impacting her attentiveness to the content of the lecture. It is almost impossible to determine in this virtual format. As the weeks of observations continue, the crochet hook and various colors of yarn appear again and again. The activity doesn't appear to detract from the student's attentiveness to the content presented in each class. The crocheting student interacts with the instructor and guest speakers as regularly as any of the students do. She wonders what the student is making. It would be interesting to see some finished projects as this student often crochets.

First Day, Take Two: Zoom Edition

She struggles with the technology and finally gets into Zoom on her phone. There is silence in the room. Two minutes pass. The instructor begins class and explains his requirement that students have their cameras turned on for participation credit. She tries to log on to call on her laptop computer (as opposed to her phone), and the Zoom room is locked. She imagines that's no different from the physical classroom of the prior year.

The instructor shares his screen to review the syllabus. He invites students to log into the course management system to look at the syllabus with him. He explains how he would like for students to address him. He lets students know that texting is permitted as he literally sleeps with his phone. Phone calls on the other hand are not permitted unless they are previously scheduled.

For students to be successful in this class, the instructor encourages them to check their email and the course management system a minimum of once daily. He also states that students must have a computer or laptop for this course. And they should take notes throughout class. He adds, "I cannot force you to read in advance, but those students who read for class typically make an A or B. And you will have to earn a C in this course for your major."

The instructor acknowledges that this is his first time teaching a synchronous class via the Zoom platform. He shares his concern that course discussion and student questions will be more challenging for him to facilitate than in a face-to-face class. He goes on to explain that the course will be mostly lecture with him stopping for more interactive moments. He admonishes students not to be distracting or he will remove them from the Zoom room. He continues on to say, "Let me know if you're going to miss class—I'm an understanding person. If I consider the circumstance to be extraordinary, I will work with you."

Everyone's cameras seem to be on.

The instructor points out that he will *not* help students with Zoom problems during the class. Rather, they should contact IT. He sums up the syllabus review saying, "You're staying in this course is your agreement to abide by the guidelines that I have set forth." He then invites students to take a minute to think about what he's gone over and to ask any questions they may have. He stops sharing his screen and notes, "You're not dismissed yet." The instructor thumbs through the students' video tiles and calls out those students whose cameras are turned off. "It's early in the morning," he remarks, "so you're probably not ready for any photo shoots, but you're looking better than I do."

The instructor tells students that he can see the chat box, but he isn't going to acknowledge comments in the chat during the class. He allows another short pause for questions. "You'll find I respond pretty quickly. I basically live with my phone, most of you do." Another pause. "Well, nice to meet you. I'm looking forward to this." The instructor points out that this course is about empathy, an important skill for those entering their intended professions. "Now more than ever," he continues, "we're dealing with something phenomenal in [your field]."

Class is dismissed twenty minutes early.

No Ambiguity

This instructor's tone is friendly, and he tries to be engaging. But it's evident that he is policy oriented. His expectations for behaviors are clear: be on time, be present, be engaged. The class sessions often begin the same way, with the instructor welcoming the students and reminding them to be visible on camera. There are what appears to be pleasant reminders to the whole class of what's expected of the students for the course: students should be sitting up, not lying down in their beds, *I shouldn't need to remind you, but I am going to remind you . . . I will call you out*; students should be visible in their cameras, *I see your wall, but I would really like to see your face*; and students should be ready to engage with the instructor and each other, *where we at folks?* Although these reminders are given to everyone, they are really directed to the same subgroup of students each week, with cameras frequently off or those who seem to prefer the comfort of their beds. For this instructor, there is a sense of professionalism that exudes a sense that they are here to support student learning, but in a no-nonsense manner that makes boundaries and expectations for behavior clear: *if [you're] not doing it in an in-person class, then you shouldn't be doing it on Zoom.*

Value As Affirmation

In current American higher education spacetimes, value returns the world through measurement. Value is a calculation; higher education research and practice values student success algorithms, cost-benefit analyses of time to degree, the cost of an additional major or minor, the human capital persons and countries gain through higher education, and so on.[2] When the value of higher education is understood through calculation, the work of education at the university becomes the work of earning credits, and the responsibility of the university is to minimize wasted credits. In such a system of values, to be recognized as a good student is to be recognizable as a proper combination of data points or dividuals,[3] to be properly spreadsheetable, databased, computable, and algorithmitized.[4]

Researchers and practitioners can and must come to value higher education in excess of measurement. There is no future beyond neoliberalism that isn't also beyond our equation of measurement with knowledge and calculation with value. Value as and through affirmation provides a path for thinking of value beyond measurement. For Gilles Deleuze, affirmation is a dice throw that contains all enumerable possibilities as well as pure chance, and each repeated result is a singularity.[5] Value as affirmation does not answer questions of value; it is rather a continual experimentation with the limits and expressions of value.[6]

Value as affirmation does not seek to bound and make discrete. Value as affirmation seeks relentless experimentation and attunement to the imperceptible: the unexpected and unrecognizable singularities emitted from repetition. This is the spirit of *The L Word* theme song: "talking, laughing, loving, breathing / fighting, fucking, crying, drinking / riding, winning, losing, cheating / kissing, thinking, dreaming."[7] This is an affirmation of lesbians—an active valuation of lesbian that doesn't rely on defining lesbians by enumerating attributes and thus bounding an inside and an outside. These are not attributes: these are expressions, each its own throw of the dice, each singular. An affirmation of the value of higher education takes on this dice throw—a repetition of attempts at gradual betterment that expresses itself differently each time, with the chance of the world tucked in each throw, each next moment open to difference.

Chat(ter)

8:43 a.m. The instructor says to the class, "I think I've covered what's most important for the quiz. Let's do this. Is there anyone who doesn't like to speak who'd like to say something? Any questions about chapter 9. Nobody? Everybody's an expert on chapter 9? Okay, I'll just give you a quiz right now. No, I'm just kidding." The instructor continues chatting. "I've gone years without filing a tax return, but that's because they owe me." One unmuted student laughs out loud. The instructor keeps asking the class questions. "What else do you have going on beside this class?" A second student shares she has lots of exams going on. The instructor asks if students plan to stay home after Thanksgiving. A third student replies saying students are permitted to stay in their residence halls.

Meanwhile, in the chat box:

From student2 to Everyone: 08:48 AM: No questions

From student3 to Everyone: 08:48 AM: what's ur cats name lol

From student4 to Everyone: 08:48 AM: how do big corporations avoid taxes? Like Amazon.

Talk to Me

The instructor opens the Zoom session for students and welcomes students to class: *How are we this fine Thursday?* There is no response from students. The instructor attempts to coax conversation: *come on, I need someone to talk to me.* Microphones remain muted, and awkward silence ensues. How do instructors draw students into discussions rather than leading classes lecture style, where information flows in a one-way direction?

It's the fifth week of classes, and the instructor wants the students to know everyone is in the same situation: if *we were all in the same room, we'd all be talking about this together, so it's good to be talking about this with each other now.* It seems to be challenging to establish a sense of community in a virtual environment. From her observation, these instructors are doing what they can to help the students feel connected to each other and the State U. community.

In Contrast

The instructor starts each class session with a fun question such as what's your favorite ice cream toppings, what are your desired superpowers, or who would you invite to a dinner party. The instructor is friendly and engaging, like other instructors at State U., but she also appears to be laid back and approachable. It's a one-credit course, and the class is meant to support students, not trip them up. *I want this to be a fun experience.* Each week as she observes the class, this instructor appears unflappable and supportive, and they assume a mentor role with students. She sets the expectations about the class and participation on the first day and sends reminders to individual students privately. There are different leadership and teaching styles among instructors, but they share student success in its broadest meaning as a common goal.

The Design Canvas

10:34 a.m. The workshop facilitators encourage learning community faculty to consider nine prompts when designing their learning communities for the following semester. The nine prompts are arranged in a matrix. The matrix, a complex table embedded in a Google Doc, is titled *Learning Community Design Canvas.*

In the *Canvas,* she reads,

- Purpose: What's the primary purpose? Scope?

- Audience: Who are your students? How will this learning be relevant to them?

- What subjects could be connected? What are the main subjects of your content? How do they connect?

- What would the structure of your learning community look like? How will you integrate your topics in your course?

- What materials and resources would you use to teach? Tech tools? High-Impact Practices (e.g., ePortfolio, Research, Service Learning)?

- Who would teach the learning activities? Co-teach?

- How can the learning community peer mentor support student learning? How can the peer mentor help reinforce learning community concepts and guide learning community students?

- How would the students learn/experience your topics in class? What activities will support the learning? What activities will support knowledge creation?

- How might you incorporate enrichment activities (in- or out-of-class) to support the integrative course design? What are campus/local/digital resources that would enhance students' learning?

At 10:35 a.m., she joins the two faculty leaders of one learning community in a breakout room. They chat.

At 11:50 a.m., they break for lunch. Their design canvas remains empty.

Virtual Events

One of the peer mentors speaks with several of the students about their perceptions of the virtual events. Some of the students share that they really like some of the virtual events, with the panel of professionals an obvious favorite with many of the students in the learning community in attendance. However, many of the students tell the peer mentor that they want more diversity in options, recommending panels of different professionals they would like to hear from and expressing that they want more social events. Many of the virtual events are conducted in a webinar format with the speaker presenting content and occasionally asking for audience responses. She notes these events have a lecture feel and many of the students do not participate any more than they did in their regular courses. The students ache for personal contact and fun, suggesting to the peer mentor that they want movie or game nights, trips to local venues such as the zoo, or other social gatherings that are not academically focused. The peer mentors note that these events are almost impossible to organize with the social distancing requirements in place that semester, but they also look forward to providing these social experiences in upcoming semesters.

It is clear that the peer mentors wish to provide the types of social experiences the students want. One peer mentor shares that in previous years, groups of students would go to lunch after class with their peer mentor. It created a connection and personalized experience that this peer mentor desired to provide for the students in this learning community. Social distancing restrictions and an emergency online learning environment are producing a chasm between individuals that seems almost impossible to bridge.

Teaching Station

She logs into the Zoom meeting six minutes prior to the start of class. The room is silent, and all students' and the instructor's microphones are muted. Aside from her, there are forty-nine students and the instructor already present. Then sixty-four students. Most everyone has their cameras turned on. The instructor's screen is shared with a slide that says, "What's to Come?" It's the first of thirty-six slides. His video displays an empty couch in front of a gray background, poorly lit.

The instructor enters her view with a white and ginger cat. He places the cat on the back of the couch and pets it. It's a pretty cat, subjectively speaking.

At the start of class time, seventy-seven students are present in the Zoom room. One minute later, eighty-one students. Still nothing is being said. She finds the silence eerie and unnerving.

The instructor's camera turns off. A casual picture of him is displayed instead.

Three minutes into class the instructor turns his camera on and says good morning. The Zoom room is now locked with eighty-five students in attendance and five to six students absent. The instructor is seated on the couch. His hair is COVID length compared to the previous year. In 2019, he had a fairly professional haircut. A year later, after restrictions that prevented folks from getting their hair cut professionally, his hair is now beyond shoulder length.

He explains he will mute all students throughout class, but folks can unmute themselves at the end of class if they want to share. The cat is in plain view behind him on the couch. The instructor introduces the cat as Cody, his fifteen-year-old cat. The instructor has his name displayed as "Professor" followed by his last name in his Zoom tile.

The lecture begins.

Another Day, Another Zoom Room

One student is a forehead propped up by a hand, lying in a bed. The bed's headboard is made of wooden slats, so it's unlikely she is in a university residence hall. She notes how the camera frames the student, duly muted per the instructor's policies. A second student has a curtain covering a window in a darkened room. A third student is a horizontal body cocooned in a blanket that has been pulled around her head. Her eyes vacantly stare at something or maybe nothing.

It is 8:15 in the morning, and seventy-one students are here. They're logged into Zoom anyway, but who knows if they're cognitively present? A fourth student, another horizontal body. The sun is beaming through her window while she lies in bed with her eyes closed. She looks over at something, yawns, then settles back down into the mattress.

In stark contrast, the fifth student is sitting up in a brightly lit room with nice big windows. Her hair is in a ponytail, with a hair band holding back any stray flyaways. She is wearing a State U. sweatshirt and seems to be put together and studious. She takes a sip from a silver travel mug and yawns. It's early.

A sixth student, on the other hand, may not be wearing any clothes. He is another horizontal body in a bed. He rubs his eyes. Eyes now open, he rests on his pillow. The seventh student is glancing down at something, presumably her phone. She wobbles a little, in danger of falling over and going back to sleep, resting her head in her right hand. She's likely sitting in a bed, but not being in the same physical space, this can't be confirmed. The student yawns big, stretching her arms over her head. She also wears a State U. sweatshirt. She looks absolutely bored, neither smiling nor nodding like students may do in a face-to-face classroom. These seven students seem completely disconnected from the instructor, separated by cameras, computer screens, walls, space, and a pandemic.

Lather, Rinse, Repeat

1. She pulls up the document containing her field notes and logs into Zoom several minutes before class start time. The instructor typically has a waiting room enabled.

2. She notes time stamps and number of students for the first few minutes.

3. She notes the instructor's remarks before he starts the lecture.

4. She notes the topic of the day's class once screen share starts.

5. She monitors the chat.

6. She scrolls through the students' Zoom tiles.

7. In her notes, she describes the tiles left to right, noting things that glow, and those that don't.

8. She notes if the instructor stops the lecture to play a video or call on a student or ask an open-ended question.

9. She returns to her tiles. Time-permitting, she scrolls for another set of students, noting their emotions[8] and behaviors.

10. She continues to monitor the chat.

11. She captures student verbal contributions.

12. She notes highlights of the lecture or PowerPoint slides.

13. She returns to tile scrolling. Every now and then, she scrolls back to the instructor.

14. She captures instructor and student remarks post screen-share along with end of class comments.

15. She stays on Zoom while students leave.

Are They Listening?

She notes that students want to spend a lot of time in today's class talking about assignments they are to submit to the instructor. Several of the students indicate that they had difficulty with submitting the assignments, with some students noting they didn't know how or where to submit the assignment while other students indicate they had experienced technical difficulties while submitting the assignments. The instructor had previously arranged for a guest speaker to attend their class to guide the students with the expectations of the assignment and to tutor the students on the technological components necessary for the completion of the assignment. Based on the questions from the students during class today, one could assume there were several students who hadn't paid attention during those previous sessions. The instructor shares that many of the students in the class didn't submit or didn't properly submit the assignments.

Hierarchy

The assistant reports to the learning community coordinator. The learning community coordinator reports to a director. That director reports to the supervisor. Visions and decisions about the life of learning communities flow like a waterfall down the steps of the hierarchy to be disseminated to the faculty who lead the learning communities. Faculty in some departments make their own decisions, choosing their own paths around the waterfall. At times they are guided by a department chair, at other times by a departmental advisor. Sometimes they are simply guided by years of doing learning communities their way.

The supervisor, the director, the coordinator, and the assistant flow on.

Yay Zoom

She is talking with a student about the content of the one-credit class and the virtual events that were hosted by the peer mentors and advisors. The student shared that the guest speakers were helpful, particularly as the class was virtual and it was a lot easier to attend on the Zoom rather than having to go to campus.

Individual Group Work

The peer mentor is covering class on behalf of the instructor today. After an icebreaker activity, the peer mentor explains the instructions for a small group activity about campus resources and assigns students to breakout rooms.

She observes breakout room number five for its twenty-four-minute duration. There are no audible student interactions as all students remain on mute. They may be working on their assignment individually, or not at all.

One student is having a lengthy conversation with someone off camera. Another student has a calendar on the wall behind her. Under Friday "Study/Homework" is written in red.

Finally, students return to the main Zoom session room. The peer mentor leads off the discussion by saying, "I will say, IT, super helpful. They're available over the phone 24/7."

When students from the fifth group are asked about the campus resources they researched, they share their findings one by one. One student shares, "I looked up the Women's Center," and provides details about the Center. Another student says, "I looked up the Study Abroad."

She is left with questions. Did the students text each other privately to coordinate who covers which resource? Did they not coordinate at all and just randomly happen to research different campus resources? Did they choose not to speak with each other in the breakout room because they were unclear about the activity? Because they were not on speaking terms with each other? Because they were indifferent?

The peer mentor reminds students that they have a copy of the document file and tells them they can save the file and keep it as a resource beyond class.

Class Discussion

The way she has cropped the screen, she can see herself, one student, and the instructor above the instructor's screen-shared PowerPoint presentation. One click to the right and she can see three additional students. She clicks a few more times, quickly glancing at the students' faces. Some of them appear to be taking notes, with only the tops of their heads displayed as they bend over to write. One woman with long hair in a ponytail on top of her head leans back in her chair to stretch. Her facial expression is neutral. Another student, this one wearing glasses, is looking down at something invisible to the observer. She could be looking at her phone or her notes; who knows? Nothing in the chat box so far.

The course meeting is being recorded. For whom, she is unsure. Would anyone who is absent today elect to watch the class recording? The sound goes in and out at times. The instructor's cat appears to have fallen asleep.

The instructor introduces a new concept and asks for examples from class. A student suggests Black Lives Matter protests as a possible example. Another student, wearing the same yellow hoodie as on Tuesday, contributes to the conversation, but his sound is set so low she can't make out what he's saying. The instructor affirms the student's response and then asks for another contribution. Another student chimes in, saying that *people who are looting might be labeled as thugs*. The instructor nods; this is what he was looking for. He explains that labeling folks doesn't explain their behavior.

"What would make somebody go from protesting to robbing a business?" the instructor asks. One student offers, "It's the only way to make change." Lively discussion ensues with five or six additional students giving responses. There is one contribution after another, flowing together and tying into each other. Students simply unmute themselves, wait their turn, and chime in. Black folks are using the words "us" and "our." Others are using the words "they" or "the looters." Out of this back and forth and over and under, the instructor asks students who aren't speaking to mute their microphones to avoid getting acoustic feedback.

The instructor summarizes the varied student responses and ties them to the topic of today's class. He explains that the businesses being looted are owned by people from different ethnic backgrounds. Businesses are symbols of the power structure. The existing power structure relates to unattainable wealth for certain populations. In the chat, one student asks if she can be next followed by "lol." Others reply that the instructor can't see the chat during screen share. The student remains silent. The instructor thanks students for openly sharing their opinions.

The student who asked to be next in the chat finally contributes to class conversation. Other students unmute themselves, but re-mute their microphones once the instructor starts speaking again.

She scrolls through the video tiles. One more time. One student is leaning low on her hand, she looks to be almost asleep.

The lecture moves on to potholes and tax money.

Same but Different

After all students have logged off, she talks with the instructor about the impact of the change this semester to synchronous Zoom class sessions. They talk about how there are some changes from in-person learning, but many things are still the same. This instructor tells her that there are just as many students who fall asleep in the in-person classes as do in Zoom classes. The only difference is that in the in-person classes, the instructor *can go around and bang on desks*. In Zoom, they just use the chat feature to privately chat with people instead: "If you could see my chat right now. All the messages I send to students during class saying hey, if you can see this chat, you need to pay attention."

Use Resources Wisely

It's almost exam week. Today she observed one of the students' three-credit courses followed by one of the one-credit ones. There is an upcoming exam in this three-credit course, and today's session was for reviewing the course content. Attendance was optional, and many students didn't come to class. Later in one of the one-credit classes, the topic of discussion was exam preparation. In addition to a discussion about tips for studying, many students expressed concerns about their ability to pass the exam in the three-credit course. Late withdrawals, impacts of failure on GPA, pass-fail options, and grade forgiveness are topics of conversation. The instructor tries to be supportive and offers general advice to all the students. As the students express concerns about the three-credit class from earlier, she notes that many of the students who are worried about their grade on the exam didn't attend the review session.

Liberal Education as Fabulation

If radical pedagogy is "the commitment to the creation of practices that foreground how learning creates its own value,"[9] liberal education is learning that "creates its own value."[10] In higher education, the value of liberal education has been captured by various national initiatives and reconstituted through standardization and rubrics,[11] even though college and university actors are always more than the sum of their rubric parts. To engage in liberal education is to be speculative and open to transformation,[12] or to be artful and thus "actively engaged in the differential of experience in the making—art must never seek to define in advance its value."[13] To reconceptualize higher education can be to reinvest in liberal education as artful practice.

The concept of liberal education looms large over discussions of value in higher education. What would it look like to reconceptualize liberal education through critical and poststructural theories and set it loose to create new everydays? First, liberal education should not be seen as liberatory. Liberal education as an institutional practice has been, with slight variation with the times, considered a luxury for those with social and economic status since its modern provenance in the nineteenth century.[14] In a precarious time where most Americans are forced to view education through a productivity calculation[15] of how will this activity help put food on the table (in the least amount of time, for the lowest cost), liberal education is again rendered as a luxury for those with a social status that places them outside of the precariat.[16] It is also not quite unique to wish to reconceptualize liberal education. In a time where the value of liberal education is set against the precarity of life in the United States, calls abound to rethink it,[17] defend it,[18] and to develop a new paradigm for it.[19] In this environment, it seems anachronistic to cling to liberal education for its je ne sais quoi. Liberal education is a concept from a world that no longer exists and to which no progressive educator wishes to return. And yet we are committed to re/conceptualizing liberal education precisely because it's a term in wide circulation and widely valued for this je ne sais quoi that, as we argue, is a shared value of imperceptible progress.

This move to reconceptualize liberal education is not unique, it is singular. And maybe amid all the singular texts that take up this expression, something sparks. In fact, this is the work of affect. All affect means or does is spark this potential; it is "a body's capacity to affect and be affected."[20] Reconceptualizing liberal education in the terms of the ordinary attunes us not to high-impact practices or other calculable values of higher education but to the impact of ordinary practices: the very anecdotes that constitute this book. These are impacts, or sparks, that we sense in the moment and that linger with us afterward. Ordinary practices are always more than the sum of their parts. They produce outcomes insofar as they produce the world. They are sparks that open and close paths not previously considered. Liberal education does not flow from environments reverse-engineered to produce outcomes but rather from anecdotes. The question of liberal education does not concern how to build a future transformation. The question is more like: What is the transformation in the here and now? This is an unanswerable question. To be experimental, speculative, open to transformation—this is liberal education. Liberal education is not searching for and amassing the proper credits that create it: it's affirmative through and through.

Liberal education as affirmation is incompatible with regimes of accountability to outcomes, and yet paradoxically it lives in the fissures of these regimes. Liberal education is not a function of particular academic programs in the same way it's not best represented by any particular set of research procedures. *Liberal education* is not a statement in search of a countable, representable, scalable identity, but a question to be asked repeatedly without end: an affirmative question that of *what's next* with no *end* in attunement.[21] Liberal education as an affirmative *what's next* desires futures that are at odds with desires for a new normal. The artful pursuit of this affirmative question produces outcomes as a by-product but does not seek them. It seeks the value of higher education: unsatisfied, it seeks this without end.

If high-impact practices are a science of producing value(s) in higher education, ordinary impacts are the art of producing values. The value of liberal education cannot be tied to outcomes; it must only be tied to ordinary experimentations, or fabulations. As such, *liberal education is* an artful student experience. Outcomes happen. Liberal education as fabulation is nothing more than "a dramatization born of joy that composes at the limits of experience in the making."[22] Liberal education is a student, faculty, staff, and constituent higher education experience as fabulation. In a liberal education, there is no satisfying an algorithm that lines up all the right credits in all the right places. There is only more, only the *what next*, only "fighting, fucking, crying, drinking . . ."[23]

The New Engagement

She notes the distinctions among the three tiles of students displayed on her screen. In the first, the student is propped up in bed against a metal wrought-iron headboard. The woman's laptop is placed on her lap. Given her eyes are open, she appears to be awake and looking at the computer screen. She reaches over to her nightstand, grabs a coffee mug, and takes a sip. Then she sits back on her bed and looks back at the screen.

The second tile is pointed at a window. The room is dark otherwise. There is no one displayed in the video tile. Presumably the student is in a bed below the window, though it's entirely possible she stepped out to use the restroom or simply turned on her camera and left the room.

The student in the third tile is sitting in a kitchen at a table. Her room is well-lit, and she appears to be writing notes on a notepad next to her laptop. Occasionally she looks at the screen, then back over to her notebook, writing things down—maybe the definitions the instructor is going over.

She clicks to scroll her display once to the right.

A fourth student is horizontally in bed. Her face is obscured by her name on the tile. There is a white Christmas tree in the corner. The student moves occasionally, but is she in this class?

Another click to the right.

Another student seems to be sitting up on her bed in the corner of her room. She appears to be taking handwritten notes, though her body is only displayed from her chest up. She looks up at the computer screen, takes out her scrunchy, and redoes her hair into a ponytail.

She pins a different student to attune to her more closely. The student's face is captured from the nose up. On the wall beside her head hangs a collage of photos saying "class of 2020." Her eyes are moving left to right then back, likely because she is reading something on the screen. Her laptop is balanced on her knees.

Another student sits at a desk or table. She wonders if this is the new measure for Engagement? The student yawns openly. She takes a swig from a metal travel mug, then scribbles handwritten notes into a notebook on her table.

Another student is horizontal in bed.

This prompts her to scroll through all of the video tiles. She counts sixteen tiles of students who are either horizontal in bed, off screen, obscured by their names, or in a room too dark for her to observe them. Are they part of this learning community? Do they want to be?

Beneficial Extra-Curriculars

To continue to provide out-of-class learning experiences for students, the learning community at State U. designed an incentive program to encourage students to attend virtual events that were offered on campus. Students designed many of the events. Students who attended various designated events would receive one entry into a randomized drawing for various prizes, including the final, most valuable prize: a pair of brand-name Bluetooth headphones. The instructor in the one-credit course introduces the initiative program and encourages all students to attend as many of the virtual events as possible. These virtual events are designed to provide opportunities for students to participate in wider conversations about careers for their intended majors.

Distractions

Another guest speaker leads the class. The topic is service learning, and the guest is friendly and engaging. The guest asks many interesting questions, and opportunities for student response are plentiful. There is no droning lecture and no death by PowerPoint. At the close of the presentation, the guest remains in the Zoom session so that students may continue to type their questions about today's topic to them in the chat box. The instructor asks the students about a recently due assignment. Half of the class hasn't submitted the assignment, and one student says they were having trouble with assignment. The instructor reminds the students that if they are having trouble, they can reach out to the appropriate campus support personnel indicated in the link on the assignment. Eventually this conversation ends, and the instructor begins to share details about an upcoming assignment. Suddenly a computer chime is heard, followed by several more. *Are you all emailing me your e-portfolio links right now? [. . .] Ya'll, aren't even listening right now [. . .] it is rude to be emailing your professor when your professor is trying to teach you. Off the email [. . .]. Can someone who I do not have an email in my inbox from please tell the class what I just shared?*

Later, after class has ended, the instructor shares her frustrations with her and the guest speaker. She feels a sense of relief for the instructor that the guest speaker is a friend, not just a colleague. She learns that in addition to the emails, two of the students had used the private chat feature to send messages during the presentation. One of these students had requested to be able to talk about last week's class session. The instructor told her that this student had been "kicked out of class last week for sleeping in class."

Ennui, Part I

It's difficult to determine in this environment, but today some of the students almost appear bored. Students are facing the camera, but their eyes appear unfocused on what is on the screen. She doesn't see eye movement that would indicate the students are looking at the information on the PowerPoint on the instructor's shared screen. Do they feel that they already know this information? Or do they not see the value in the materials presented? During a conversation that occurred just after the midpoint of the semester, the instructor tells her that the students seem really overwhelmed. Many of the students have shared with the instructor that they are experiencing a lot of anxiety about their courses; many are quarantined, and many are tired of attending classes virtually, an experience the instructor calls "Zoom fatigue." Many of these students ended their senior year of high school in this unfamiliar emergency remote online Zoom environment, and they missed out on many of the senior-year rites of passage and now they are completing their first semester of their first year of college on Zoom. These dynamics appear to be taking a toll on the students. Are they overwhelmed?

Faculty Workshop Goals

The central learning community coordinating office for learning communities has outcomes in mind for this faculty workshop. The desired outcomes are:

- Communicate with one another to identify the "big question" or overarching concern connecting the courses;
- Connect the courses to this "big question" via an integrated assignment and activity;
- Consider how to amplify or deepen understanding of the courses' engagement with the "big question" through an enrichment activity;
- Consider how a learning community might be delivered in a virtual environment.

Zoom

The Zoom environment appears to create many challenges for instructors to set and manage expectations for students' behavior. In a classroom, an instructor may be better able to determine which students are on electronics viewing non-course-related content. It's hard to tell in this environment how frequently those distracted behaviors are occurring. How do they really monitor and manage that? How does this environment impact the students' experiences?

Random Moments

In discussing the impact of the COVID-19 pandemic on their college experience, one student said, "You know, it's already hard being your first semester in college [and] making it virtual feels like it's harder to connect with people outside in the real world."

Wonderings

As the semester continues, the instructor appears to be frustrated with the behavior of many of the students during the Zoom session. The instructor tells her that the students are not taking the class seriously and this is different from how students have not taken the course seriously in previous semesters. She wonders what the students' expectations for Zoom sessions are. Do the students view these class sessions as similar to an in-person course? Or do they feel like because they aren't physically in a classroom that anything goes with regard to behavior?

And Monotony

As the weeks go by, the monotony of observing in Zoom is increasingly evident. She has been observing four one-credit courses and as the weeks go by, it's the same checklist of items noted, the number of blank screens, students faced away from the camera, how many individuals are lying down. What does fourteen weeks of these notes tell us about student Engagement? Are students who were facing the camera more engaged than those who turned their cameras toward the ceiling or turned their cameras off? She wonders if the emergency online Zoom learning environment creates more opportunities for disengagement or if the observed behaviors this semester reflect the challenges experienced by students regardless of the learning medium. Maybe this modality of course delivery simply highlights potential disengagement through the segregated display of students and instructors, with its limited view of the wider environment in which they attend the class. Without knowledge of what is outside the camera display, the instructor, guest, or observer can only guess the meaning of the limited behaviors they see. Arm movement may mean the student is taking notes on the materials presented by the instructor or it could mean something entirely different. Black screens may indicate that the student has logged on to the class but walked away from the computer, but they also could mean that there is something happening in the student's physical environment that shouldn't be seen by the class. Faces directed toward the web camera could denote attentiveness, and they could be evidence that the student is looking at something on their computer that is completely unrelated to the course content.

Confusion

She asks one of the administrators what defines learning communities on this campus and what makes them unique.

The administrator laughs and says.

> I think I know less after seeing all the learning community teams. I thought I knew. And I don't know if it's just because the university keeps inheriting older systems of doing things. The university is designed around the principle that you should be able to synthesize content between fields, but that's not our experience. Our experience is we become masters of this really narrow bit of knowledge and the rest is kind of tacked on. I think learning communities can be the first real major shift in that where students can see not just course content, but like a really good learning community would have faculty speaking to one another, you know? Students don't see the disciplines talking to each other because they don't see the humans talking to each other, you know, and so like what if you had a question of the week? Students respond to it. And then there's a video of the two professors, saying, hey, we saw

your responses and in the field of rhetoric, we would say, blah blah blah, hey faculty X, what would biology say to that? You know, and thus, it's the students talking to us and us talking back to them. And so I think a long-winded answer there. I think a learning community is communal. I think it's really social when done well. I think it's practical in that students take the text knowledge and apply it in a new context. And I think it's integrated which you saw of course with the workshop. I think those fields or those courses need to be in meaningful conversation and not just a superficial like . . . we just happened to be tagged together. And there's an assignment that joins us in some meaningless way. Like (laughs). And honestly, like a really good learning community should have those bridges multiple times a semester very explicitly."

Some of the words and phrases the administrator used stand out to her: "would," "what if," "need to be," "should," "superficial," "meaningless." What about "useless"? Could this be a good thing?

Lecture Format, Part II

Toward the end of the term, there is a normalized flow to the lecture that reprises in each class period. She logs onto Zoom. The instructor is off screen, and the students are in the waiting room. One minute before class the instructor admits everyone to the main room. Perhaps twenty or so students are absent, and a dozen are in bed or have their camera turned off. The instructor calls on students who are asleep or off screen and removes them if they don't respond. The instructor shares his screen, and the lecture begins.

All students have muted themselves per the instructor's expectations. They sit at tables, recline in beds, or turn their cameras toward their ceilings and do other things. A few may be taking notes, but others may be replying to emails or texting, scrolling through their Instagram feeds, or watching TV. Sometimes they eat or drink, or they talk to someone off screen. They attend to personal hygiene matters, such as taking a shower or cleaning one's ears. At this point, about twenty of the forty students' Zoom tiles are dark, pointed toward anywhere but the students, or display students in bed, perhaps asleep.

With fifteen minutes to go, the instructor stops screen-sharing and asks students to unmute so they can verbally contribute to discussion prompts. A few do. It's the same few each week. The instructor dismisses class and students log off one by one. Some say thanks, and some wave. The class concludes with one or two students sleeping. The instructor attempts to wake them up but ultimately removes them from the Zoom room.

"See you again next class." Undoubtedly, for more of the same.

Zoning Out

It is hard to observe the students as she is limited by the course delivery medium. The behaviors visible within the tiles on the screen offer limited insights into what the students are doing. There is a guest speaker in class today. She notes that a student glances back and forth between the screen and something in front of the student; the student keeps looking down. She wonders if the student is working on homework or other classwork while the guest speaker is presenting. She also notes that there is a student looking to the right. She catches a brief glimpse of an object in the student's right hand and wonders if the student is looking at a phone. As the class continues, she wonders if the students are attentive to the content being presented. It's hard to make definitive determinations in this environment, but it appears as though students aren't attentive; they are physically present but not engaged. There are a lot of eyes looking down or away from the screen, slouched bodies, and eyes closed. If she were asked to interpret the behaviors she observed today, she would guess that students were bored or uninterested.

Reflection

At the end of the semester, the instructor of the one-credit course had planned to provide time for the students to discuss their experiences with the peer mentor. The instructor's camera is turned off, and the peer mentor asks the students to unmute and share. At first, the students are quiet. When asked about the one-credit course, one of the students responds, "I liked that we could talk to each other and get to know each other a little more because we really couldn't do that in our other classes. Especially since it was hard to join clubs." The inability to participate in typical in-person college activities was noticeably difficult for these students whose world changed radically months before. Another student says, "Can I add on to that? I wish I could have participated in more sports . . . it's hard because I am not actually on campus and no one would really meet with me."

The peer mentor asks the students to share their thoughts on any of the virtual events the students attended. One of the students says, "Yeah, I liked them. I found them helpful. I like to learn things on my own, but I also liked to hear from other people." The conversation about the virtual events continues with students sharing some of the virtual events they enjoyed. The peer mentor reminds the students that one of their classmates won the biggest prize in the incentive program. The discussion shifts to suggestions that the students may have for events in future semesters. There are suggestions for events that highlight a broader range of majors, but most of the suggestions center on the students' desire to have more in-person events. She notes that this class is normally very quiet, so the ten minutes of conversation between the peer mentor and the students is a little unexpected. Conversation bubbles and percolates, particularly between the peer mentor and four specific students. The student input is refreshingly honest, providing evidence that this semester of virtual classes and restricted contact with other students was quite challenging.

Musings

The instructor addresses the students lying in beds and clarifies the expectations for students' behavior while in class sessions. She emphasizes that students should be sitting up, taking notes, and being attentive to the instructor or any guest leader of the class. She reminds students that guest speakers will be coming to class, indicating that students in bed create a negative perception. To enforce expectations of attentiveness and engagement, the instructor indicates that in the future students will lose attendance points if they are lying in bed. Despite reiterations of these expectations and warning of repercussions for students who don't adhere to them, students continue to have their cameras off or pointed at the ceiling during class sessions. Are these students engaged? Are they listening? Are they learning?

What's the Buzz?

The buzz that had permeated the classrooms of the prior year has been suppressed by muted microphones, vacant cameras, and empty chat boxes. Students don't write or speak within the Zoom environment, disconnected from the bi-directional forces that connect them. The buzz appears to have been extinguished, blown out by the bits and bytes of videoconferencing technology. What they don't know is whether this buzz is still aflame through group texts or social media messaging apps. Perhaps there are dorm room gatherings and whispers about learning and engagement in the hallways of the residence halls. Perhaps there is a GroupMe that's just popping off day and night. Or perhaps still bodies and vacant glances into video cameras are a new type of buzz of their own.

In Zoomland, the buzz is ever becoming.

Environmental Awareness

Homes and dorms rooms have become multipurpose: bedrooms, dining rooms, classrooms. Day in and day out, the students attend from confined spaces, limited by social distancing and restrictions. They become comfortable, maybe too comfortable, within their same four walls. Lives lived do not stop because someone has yet another Zoom class. Humans pass by, dogs want attention, someone is wrapped in a blanket yet again, and so on. It's just another day and the students dutifully have their cameras on as they have been told they must. Most days, the visuals within the Zoom tiles are benign, inconsequential, or uninteresting. But some days, she is shocked.

As she scans through the Zoom tiles, one student briefly captures her attention. The student is facing the camera, attending to the day's lecture; nothing special there. It's the background that gives her pause. A person in the background emerges from behind a door, wrapped in a bath towel and, one can assume, nothing else. Does the instructor observe this, too? The moment is noted and passes, the lecture continues. The instructor mentions nothing. The next week, the instructor welcomes students to the class in the usual way. As part of the greeting, she acknowledges the moment from the last class session, nonchalantly and professionally, *If you all can do me a favor, please make sure I can see you in the camera view [. . .] make sure you are aware of your surroundings and what's going on in the background.*

To Value the Useless

Anecdotes strung together ad infinitum might seem like a useless project to pursue—and that, if so, would be a compliment. Valuing the ordinary, or more precisely attuning to the value of the ordinary, is to attune to practices that live within and are overdetermined by quantification.[24] It is to attune to practices and anecdotes that we might otherwise label useless. If the anecdotes express practices, or the location of liberal education, we must come to value anecdotes. In so doing, we value the useless.

Valuing higher education as useless may be anathema to data-driven culture, but it isn't new.[25] To be useless is to have no outside aim or value defined in advance.[26] To paraphrase NeNe Leakes, *its use is its use.*[27] This isn't a thought exclusive to the realm of academic scholarship. For Arcade Fire, to value the ordinary comes in part from valuing wasted time:

> All those wasted hours we used to know
> Spent the summer staring out the window
> The wind it takes you where it wants to go . . .
> Wasted hours, before we knew
> Where to go, and what to do
> Wasted hours that you make new
> And turn into
> A life that we can live.[28]

To value the ordinary is to value the now in all of its messy potential, in all of its waste—or—potential connection to our tangible aspirations. To be useless is to live this value and live in affirmation. To spotlight the useless within a high-impact practice is the paradoxical intervention this book makes. Valuing the useless produces "a life that we can live."[29] Liberal education is attunement without end. To value the useless is to attune to imperceptible progress, and when it becomes perceptible, attuning again to the imperceptible. To value the useless in university classroom life is to live a liberal education and to revalue higher education one anecdote at a time. In these ordinary revaluations, we create the conditions for college environments in the aftermath of neoliberalism and its attendant attempted optimizations of campus life.

Study Hall

This class section includes the guaranteed entry students, so the assumption is that these students are higher-achieving students and are more likely to be engaged in classes. While she notes some of the behaviors observed in other one-credit course sections in this class, such as having a visitor in bed, there are student behaviors that are evident across all course sections: lying in bed, being only partially visible on camera, looking at phones, completing other tasks during the synchronous session, or talking to roommates or other individuals in students' physical environment while the instructor or guest speaker is speaking. For some of the students, the one-credit class may be viewed as a time to work on homework from another class. Maybe they don't see the course as valuable. It's difficult to tell in this environment, but the students consistently appear to demonstrate behaviors that seem to indicate lack of attentiveness. Would they engage in these behaviors if this class were being held in an in-person classroom?

Defining Engagement

Perhaps there is no common definition of engagement at this university. Maybe the definition is a compilation of individual definitions.

Faculty 1:

> We love to use that term, right? And what does that mean? Yeah, yeah, I'm going to fail you here because I don't have a sexy definition like. It's that feeling of . . . or, like, you know it when you see it, right? I feel like I talk about student engagement when there is enthusiasm, which is I know an unquantifiable thing. Really all Likert scales in the world don't help us. But when I see students taking a thing and owning it . . . making it more than I could have designed for, you know, a lot of my

work is often just setting the stage and letting people go, like, see where they go with it. I think student engagement is when you see them enthusiastically grappling with the concepts and demonstrating not mastery, inherently, you know? Like I always have trouble with that term, but the desire to master that, or apply it elsewhere and . . . just . . . active is I think the word I derive in the end, like student engagement is not a student listening for three hours and then regurgitating it back to you, even if they have a grade of 100. I don't inherently think that student was engaged, you know, so. I don't know. Now I'm going to have to go do research.

Faculty 2:

Student engagement. Okay, so anything that they are actually like, okay, you know, "I'm excited to actually go to a student organization that's relevant to my major and like you know make these connections with other people to get a little bit more knowledge than I would if I hadn't." You know? So anything that they, they're like, okay, "I'm going to do an internship as a result of this" or are you gonna, you know, do some research with a faculty member? So, really I think it's kind of like a contagion thing. So, they're open to like participating in other experiences that are going to maximize their success. So, really that's what engagement is, I think.

Faculty 3:

It's a jargon-y kind of thing. Right? It's a buzzword. But what is it? Student engagement, as I see it might not be the way that the university defines it, right? But what I'm thinking of and what I'm constantly looking for in the trajectory of students, not only in our class, but kind of in their tenure at [State U.], is that they get some kind of help with integrative learning. Meaning, what are you supposed to be doing with this knowledge once you leave the classroom? Right? How do I help you understand what's in it for you? And that's what I mean by student engagement. I think about what's in it for you? Because then that'll do a whole lot more for it latching on in the brain. And then, actually, you know, working toward it seriously and then using it later on. Also, for students, you know, one of the things that gets overlooked a whole lot, but something that comes back in the research and something that I think about is the fact that, you know, the things that we sometimes think of as being most important for retention and engagement is not like, you know, students getting good grades or having the best experience. It's often one mentor that they have. If they have like, if they develop a real kind of mentorship relationship with someone. And that might, you know, be linked to more like undergraduate research, like how do you guide students in learning types of things. And so, when I think of student engagement, I think of experiences that help students learn about what they might be asked to do in their field in the real world, in their discipline at large. And how they can utilize that information and continue to use it beyond the class.

Chapter Four

Engagement (2019–20)

Expectation versus Reality

"Y'all, I expected college to be like the movie *Stomp the Yard*. And then when I got here, I realized that it wasn't!" The peer mentor leads the class of quiet first-year students through an exercise in sharing. A few students chuckle at her outrage. They had spent five minutes in contemplative silence to write down five expectations they had of college, as well as five realities they had encountered during their first three weeks here.

The peer mentor asks each student to share one of their expectations and one of their realities. At the peer mentor's request, students respond in the order in which they are seated.

"I thought I'd have to study a lot, but I haven't studied once." She sees a few heads nod in response.

The peer mentor nods to the next student. "I expected that it was going to be hard to meet people, but I already know people all around campus and they come up and say hey."

"Food," the student sitting behind her chimes in. "The food here is nasty, I'm sorry." This generates some raucous reactions from her classmates.

"I thought I would like commuting and I don't," adds another student. Most of the students in the class live on campus, so there is little reaction to this statement.

Another female student goes next. "I thought I was going to like the weather, but the humidity is messing with my hair, and I can't really do that, and my allergies have gotten worse." The peer mentor smiles in sympathy.

"Man, I thought I would like parties, but I actually hate them . . . my life is in danger." Students talk over each other in response. The person sharing grumbles, "I didn't even know where I was!"

Parties appear to be a theme. She is somewhat surprised that students are honest about their experiences with alcohol-related social life in front of the instructor. Then again, there was talk about a party on Main Street during class the week before, with the instructor asking about jungle juice.

Along those lines, another student shares that he "thought the parties were going to be a little wilder." His neighbor adds, "I thought I was going to be a social butterfly, but most of the parties here get shut down in like thirty minutes." Nodding heads and general groaning are signs that the learning community agrees with this disappointing assessment.

The next student inadvertently steers the conversation back to an academic topic. "I haven't gotten a grade in a single class and I'm waiting for something to hit me in the back and kill me." It was an opportunity for the peer mentor to chime in and, well, *peer mentor*. The opportunity floats away like an autumn leaf on a babbling brook.

"I nap at least once a day." This isn't prefaced by an expectation. This is simply the student's reality.

"My expectation was I was going to go to the gym because I live in [this residence hall] and it's like right there, but instead I just eat. I'm about to gain fifteen pounds." This appears to ring true for several students. Others chuckle in response.

The peer mentor takes back the reins from the class and shares tips for how to succeed in college.

Her mind is still on jungle juice and students thinking their lives are in danger. She wonders where the students' minds are.

Planning Meeting

The focus of this meeting is to plan for the first faculty workshop. What makes learning communities unique at State U.? A joined theme, one or more integrated assignments, and a Big Question.

[3:10 supervisor turns off video]

There is discussion about conducting out-of-class activities during the time of COVID-19. Examples of virtual activities will be shared with faculty to assist in planning.

[3:16 supervisor turns on video]

"You're still going to have a few overachievers who are going to be a little panicked. Am I right in that? I think it's better to just give them a stripped-down agenda."

One of the facilitators in the room recommends sending agenda and zoom links instead, so it's a compact email with not too many distractors. *You want to scaffold the release of information. We want to model what we want them to in their courses as well.*

[3:20 supervisor turns off video]

Meeting facilitator plans to reference the two staff members who are currently out of the office.

["Is it necessary to mention them?
You might get questions about what is their role."]

Meeting facilitator justifies her mentioning them. She goes on to say she plans drop the link to the resources for faculty folder in the chat during the workshop.

["Why do you need to drop the folder?
They already have access to it on the slide."]

Another staff member comes to the facilitator's rescue: "I recommend giving multiple points of entry for online content and think we should also send a follow up email on June 3."

One staff member shares her example of an integrated assignment: Dr. Seuss rapping over Dr. Dre. Two team members smile in response.

[3:34 supervisor leaves meeting]

The practice presentation run-through continues. They are assigned to breakout rooms so the facilitator can practice doing this.

[3:35 supervisor rejoins meeting]

They return from their breakout rooms.

[3:38 supervisor is standing/walking, video is shaky. Video is turned off]

[The supervisor is no longer on the call.]

Student Engagement, Let Me Count the Ways

One instructor relates a story of a student who was genuinely interested in helping low-income women receive feminine hygiene products free of charge. She explains, *I was able to help the student see how they can become socially engaged and become engaged through my class in the community in our area. You know, a community engagement, I guess.*
    #1 Community engagement.

———

Another instructor shares that for him one of the highlights of student engagement was out-of-class events. *If you do them early enough,* he elaborates, *then it increases the rapport you have with them, and the bonding.*
    #2 Bonding with faculty.

———

But for many faculty, student Engagement relates to classroom behavior. Agreeing with this point, a third instructor chimes in: *I think just their overall involvement in the class. One of the ways that I tried to find out if students had done the reading was to ask questions and point to specific parts of the chapter. I mentioned specific things from the textbook to see if they would connect, you know, and if students were able to respond appropriately, then I have the feeling that they had actually done the reading. I think that was one of the things that pointed to my belief that they were engaged. They were doing the readings on a weekly basis.*

#3 Completion of homework assignments.

———

For some faculty, it helps to sound out the word Engagement to truly grasp its meaning. *Engagement. Engagement. Yeah. So, I think the engagement was happening. I think they all engage with each other well. And so, then they engage with the class. Yeah, I think that's all I can say about that because I know there are different definitions of engagement, but in my class, engagement is just like participation. Right? It's participation. And so, I think they all did that pretty well. I didn't have to force it.*

#4 Class participation.

———

Engagement is more about the team assignment and inside classroom discussions, another instructor asserts. *Discussion, yes. But the important thing was creating a presentation and giving a speech about that presentation as a group.*

#5 Class discussion and groupwork.

———

For yet other learning community faculty, student Engagement has little to do with the classroom. One of them adds, *I think they were engaged with each other pretty well, at least in the smaller class section I had, which is important. I think there probably was like some cliqueiness and some things, but no group of humans can get away from that.*

#6 Sense of community.

———

Ordinary Thursday

Four minutes prior to the start of class, students are waiting in the hallway. Waiting for the instructor to come. Waiting for the classroom to be unlocked. Animatedly chatting with each other about who knows what.

The instructor arrives and unlocks the door. Students file into the classroom, and conversation ceases as they cross the threshold. Students sit down quietly at their desks and pull out their cellphones to start scrolling.

This room has individual chair-desks on wheels, and it consistently looks like a mess when they enter class, with chair-desks askew. They walk in today to a different arrangement: it's actually orderly. Someone has straightened up the chair-desks in the room.

At 9:30 a.m., the instructor begins class by saying, "Are there just less of you today? This looks like a good day to take roll." One student scoffs. Attendance is 22 out of 24. Maybe the straightening up and spreading out of the desks makes the room look emptier than it is. The instructor passes a sign-in sheet to the first student on the right side of the room. He also prompts students to put away electronic devices. There is a general shuffle as students tuck away their phones.

"Who's been through a hurricane before?" The instructor's question prompts a raising of hands by half the class. He goes on to quip about taking out his canoe that weekend because the area where he lives commonly floods. There is no audible response from the class.

In the span of five minutes, the locus of conversation shifted from the students to the instructor. It doesn't shift back at the end of class.

Documenting Effective Educational Practices

George Kuh and collaborators are clear about the role of student engagement in what they call "effective educational practices."[1] Student engagement is the glue that binds institutional practice to student satisfaction, student learning and development, and persistence. Student engagement has two components that practitioners and administrators should note. The first component is student time and effort.[2] The locus of control for the first component is inside individual students. This makes it not terribly interesting from an institutional perspective when thinking about current students, as it's something that institutions can only indirectly affect.

The second component of student engagement is where institutions can and should act. This component "is the ways the institution allocates resources and organizes learning opportunities and services to induce students to participate in and benefit from such activities."[3] This is the item that institutions can change, and when they do this part well, they can indirectly impact the first component: "if faculty and administrators use principles of good practice to arrange the curriculum and other aspects of the college experience, students would ostensibly put forth more effort. Students would write more papers, read more books, meet more frequently with faculty and peers, and use information technology appropriately, all of which would result in greater gains in such areas as critical thinking, problem solving, effective communication, and responsible citizenship."[4] When this is the frame, the question becomes: What works? What are these institutional practices that can influence student time and effort on task, thus increasing student engagement and increasing student satisfaction, student learning and development, and student persistence?[5] The student experience, along with staff and faculty practice, become objects of optimization. It isn't just that there needs to be more student engagement, and thus more attention and action to good practice by staff and faculty: to produce quality student engagement, staff and faculty must engage in proper sets of good practice at the right times. This is a routinized student experience designed to produce students at optimized levels of satisfaction, learning, and persistence.[6] The logic is so commonplace in American higher education as to be banal. This logic leads to projects of not just "Documenting Effective Educational Practices,"[7] but routing educational practices to the effective, timing educational practices when most effective, seeking out feedback on institutional feedback more rapidly in order to better route educational practices. This logic is additive; there is always something more to do in order to be a responsible institutional actor. This logic is colonizing: there is no area of university practice that can be responsibly left outside this logic. More engagement leads to more consumption of an academic environment. Better consumption of an academic environment is better engagement.

For They Rest

10:23 a.m. One student is trying really hard not to fall asleep.

The instructor lectures about observation as a method of data collection. He continues to work through the PowerPoint slides displayed on the screens at the front of the room. Aside from one-word answer responses to his questions, the instructor has been lecturing for about fifteen minutes. "I watch Netflix a whole lot, probably too much," he says. One student laughs out loud.

10:35 a.m. The student who struggled to stay awake is now asleep.

Ironically, during a lecture on observation as data collection, the instructor either doesn't notice the sleeping student or ignores him. "What is ethics?" he asks. Two students respond with their best guess.

10:40 a.m. Asleep student wakes up and takes a picture of the current slide.

10:42 a.m. Asleep student is asleep again.

Laying Down the Law

It is the fifth week of class. The instructor begins class by calling the roll. Students call out "here" whenever their name is called. The instructor then alerts students that she will now enforce the university attendance policy with no students admitted to the class ten minutes after the hour. Students shift in their chairs. Five minutes after class starts, one student arrives late. The instructor ignores this. Six minutes later, two other students arrive. Again, the instructor says nothing, except to continue carrying on with her lecture.

The next day, the learning community's peer mentor asks her about this class. She shares the instructor's announcement of the attendance policy. "Oh yeah," he replies. "I saw that on the GroupMe." *The students were texting those who were absent, urging them to hurry to class before the professor locked the door.*

Community.

Twenty-One Shades of Gray

Another day, another learning community class. The room is quiet, both in color and sound. The walls are white; the floor is gray. The desk chairs are black. The lights are dimmed. Students are quietly scrolling on their phones as they wait for the instructor to start class. It is monochromatic and muted.

All but three of the students wear tops in varying shades of gray, from white to black. Two students are wearing shirts in dark maroon, the color of a Japanese maple tree. But there is one burst of color: a student with pink hair who is wearing a pink shirt and a yellow knit hat. She stands out like a unicorn among horses. Is she part of this community?

The student closest to her is wearing a gray sweatshirt with the hood pulled up on her head. Her nails are painted black. Her notebook has a gray cover, but her pens write in a rainbow array of colors. She appears to be trying to tune out her surroundings, protecting herself with her hood to the point where it seems like she is checked out. Is she part of this community?

The instructor sits at the desk in the front of the classroom. He is wearing his typical khakis and t-shirt. The clothes are youthful and don't read faculty member. The color palette of his outfit fits that of the class with its muted tones. Most of the students aren't making eye contact with him or speaking with him until he starts class. Is he part of this community?

Fractured Structuring Devices

A massified and bounded impact set in stone after the experience in question occurs leaves room for the world to escape. Student Engagement and Integrative Learning as structuring devices overdetermine campus life.[8] As concepts thought to be so important for measurable outcomes, we need additional values of Engagement and Integration so that we may also speak to—and create—generative community and individual-building spaces at the core of educational projects. For Kathleen Stewart, "a still life is a static state filled with vibratory motion, or resonance. A quivering in the stability of a category or a trajectory, it gives the ordinary the charge of an unfolding."[9] Through narrating the ordinary impacts within learning community coursework through anecdote, we draw out the vibratory motions of student engagement and integrative learning.

These vibratory motions are here, now. We need not wait for a time after in which they can be produced as impact.

Not Out of the Ordinary

The topic switches to time management. As usual, the room is dark, packed with students, and (un)comfortably warm. A student in the back row is leaned back in his chair, asleep.

The peer mentor splits today's class of twenty-two into groups of four students each to work on an activity related to time management. This is a timely topic for week five of the first semester of college. She passes out sheets with instructions for the activity. Students read the scenario of a student struggling with just this issue out loud. A few minutes pass. Two of the groups are working on the assignment, but the other two groups appear to be talking about unrelated things. Perhaps they are struggling with time management.

With four minutes remaining to work on the activity, all of the groups appear to be finished. Unaware of this, the instructor announces two more minutes of time. The students are boisterous and no longer working on the activity. The instructor and the peer mentor are chatting at the front of the room. The students are loudly chatting in the middle of the room. She is in the back of the room pondering the purpose of all this chatting. Perhaps community? Perhaps Engagement? Perhaps neither.

The peer mentor facilitates the groups' report-out, and the instructor occasionally chimes in with additional advice.

One student remarks, "Bad study habits, poor sleep schedule, poor eating habits . . . story of my life right now." The comment passes without acknowledgment from the instructor, but there are nods and chuckles from his fellow classmates. Story of his life. Story of their lives?

With five minutes to go, students start packing up. This is quite late for the traditional pack-up schedule. The instructor exclaims, "Hold on a second!" Her specific remarks get lost in the shuffle of backpacks and coats. Two minutes later, class concludes and students immediately get up and walk out.

Insight Out

" 'The university needs to tell us what's happening in the fall,' one of the faculty members said just as I jumped into their breakout room, and I had to redirect their conversation."

It's five minutes after the conclusion of Day 1 of the faculty workshop, and learning community administrators are debriefing the session and planning for Day 2. The atmosphere in the Zoom call is a mixture of cheerful, relieved, and intense. It's a complex combination of vibes coming from the planning team members. The meeting appears to be collaborative, with no real leader emerging.

One of the facilitators mentions that an instructor told her there was confusion about who was teaching one of the learning communities in the fall. Another chimes in, "Yes, and some of them didn't know who their group mates were."

One of the administrators rolls her eyes. "What else do you want me to do? They've been told. We told them right when we introduced them to their peer mentors."

She learns that twenty-five out of forty or so faculty had already completed their end-of-workshop surveys. "There's a lot of goodwill that's showing up in these Qualtrics," one of the administrators sums up the responses. The conversation continues:

We need to trim up talking.

We need to give them more time to work on their worksheet.

We need to assign facilitators to their first breakout room immediately.

We need to be the experts in the room.

We need to address the anxiety by having a plan.

We need to redirect them to talk about learning communities, not just online teaching.

As the meeting concludes, one of the staff members summarizes, "We got them launched and most of the responses were positive. Negative nellies are the ones you anticipate."

Another agrees. "They didn't throw rocks at us, so . . ." The team gives each other socially-distanced high fives.

She wonders what the faculty really think.

College Wisdom

The peer mentor explains that for her, being successful means "actually reaching my goals." She goes on to share tips for how the students can be successful, too.

"Take good notes. Take advantage of your resources. Be aware that what you do now is going to impact the rest of your life."

The students stare at her. Most of their looks are blank. Some of them may be absorbing the information, but it's difficult to be sure.

"Make a plan. If you want to party, get your work done early. Don't procrastinate."

The instructor chimes in to say that faculty expect students to follow rules. The peer mentor continues with her motivational speech. "Stay on top of your work!" She offers a study session that evening for a quiz in one of their classes tomorrow. She plans to send out an email with more information. This is one of the resources she mentioned. She wonders how many of them will take advantage of it.

Engagement, a Student's Point of View

She asks a learning community alumna about her engagement with her learning community classes last fall.

> I actually feel like it was the perfect opportunity because we all ended up becoming friends like we went on our introduction to the [college] class we had like a little, a little field trip together so it like bonded us together as friends. And then in a lot of the classes when we have like group projects and stuff we decided to work together. So, it, it was really nice because it bonded us and we were able to find other people in our classes who, you know, we're coming from the same pathway that we were coming from. . . . like with the opportunities it's made me feel more engaged because we're . . . like we, you get that sense of doing it together and the [learning community] does put those opportunities out there for you to get to know your field outside of just what you're learning in the classroom. So, you get that opportunity to apply it. So that makes you feel more engaged in and makes you feel more eager to do your work. Or find your purpose, because I do know some students from the [learning community] that have learned a little more about the [field of study] world and now have switched over to different majors, so we're able to get that firsthand experience that way we can decide now as a freshman, than studying [field of study] for three years and then switching your major your junior year, because that can be very stressful.

Logistics

It's late on a Friday afternoon in June. They run through the presentation for the faculty workshop on Zoom for the following Tuesday. One of the presenters has scripted statements, others speak without notes. The graduate assistant practices placing relevant links in the meeting chat feature. The presentation slides appear ready.

They practice assigning participants into breakout rooms. Half of the team members get stuck in the main room. Preassigning breakout rooms only works when participants sign on with the correct email address. Finally, all are assigned and cohosts practice jumping between rooms.

As the meeting wraps, a list of to-dos is sent through the chat: (1) clean copy of the agenda; (2) phone numbers for during workshop texts; (3) review end-of-workshop survey and trigger email. "Monday for everything—just to have it done," suggests one facilitator.

"It's going to be Zoom polished," says another.

One facilitator asks, "I'm going to give you a request to not be in one breakout room in particular, but I'll email you that." The host of the meeting isn't surprised. Another facilitator turns her camera back on. "I was switching devices . . . but those are my peeps, I'll take that room!"

"Hands in, we did it!" Participants hold one hand out to their respective cameras, then raise it in celebration like a hands-in circle.

The host concludes the meeting. "Happy Friday, everyone!"

A Pin Drop

A student walks into the lecture hall twelve minutes late. The other students are silent. The instructor stops his announcements and watches the student walk to her row, and to her seat. Words are exchanged between the instructor and student.

The instructor asks, with an edge: "Hey how's it going?"

The student responds with a mix of surprise and saltiness, and without deference: "Sup?"

He continues with the edge in his voice: "How you feelin'? Are you okay?"

"No."

"Did you hit traffic? Bridge?" She asks herself why is this still going on?

The student seems irritated. She tries to put an end to this: "I don't have no problem."

The instructor just can't let it go: I was able to get here on time.

"Good for you."

A low, low buzz begins. It's a nervous buzz, not loud but most certainly audible, palpable.

"You'll need to see me after class." He pauses. "Life happens, and seventy other people are in here right now." Another pause. The buzz tapers off. The instructor returns to his announcements. *Last quiz—mostly As—great job. Happy with the turnout at the class event.* "Other than one or two of you who were a little belligerent and misbehaved, the rest of you did very well. We'll have to remember that because we're going [on a field trip], and that's out in public." A small buzz of low laughter bubbles up here. This strikes her as an odd comment given the mood in the room. He pulls up his slides to begin the lecture.

Before he begins, he has one last housekeeping item: "For those of you who can go on Saturday, show of hands if you have a car and are willing to be a taxi." Three, then four hands go up. "Okay, good." *There's a game Saturday. Sunday we're getting busses, but Saturday we're just getting vans, which is fine, but as of right now we're not getting enough.*

He begins his lecture. You can hear a pin drop in here. He has asked no side questions yet to class, it's all him talking from/with/to/at his slides.

What Does Affect Do?

Affect within affect theory[10] carries a particular definition: it is an intra- and extra-personal intensity that carries "multiple and normally mutually exclusive potentials, only one of which is 'selected.'"[11] Affect as such carries both realities that come into being and potential realities that do not actualize. Intensity here refers to capacities to move and be moved—capacities that may be incited by sound or other senses.[12] Affect—distinct from emotion, an intra-personal state—is thus a posthuman construct, or a construct that decenters the individualized human subject and centers our constitution as subjects from the social.[13] Affect creates us as we come to know ourselves as individuals.

Affect theory gives practitioners, researchers, and administrators one path to complicating structuring devices such as student engagement, integrative learning, and impact. Affect resists representation and quantification. Affect produces the anecdotes of student experience.[14] These are the anecdotes that are unaccounted for in traditional empirical research that discounts anecdote as nonscientific[15] and presumes students to be individualized and measurable entities.[16] Affect as such isn't subsumable within structuring devices like student Engagement whose measurements rely on individualized and measurable students.[17] This is not to say that affect is absent in structuring devices, as it is present through and through. It is to say that affect exceeds them. Affect accounts for social environments as radically constitutive of the students we come to measure.

Student engagement has a long history in the higher education and student affairs literature[18] as well as a prominent positioning in recent literature as the keystone concept in the production of student success.[19] While there is no single definition of student engagement, it's often defined as both an individual and institutional construct: the time and effort students devote to college experiences and institutional commitments to encourage such activities.[20] Across these uses, student engagement is an intra-personal or intra-institutional measurement. This book resonates instead with Macfarlane and Tomlinson's thoughts toward critical approaches to student engagement.[21] Whereas Macfarlane and Tomlinson conclude with a call for critical research that advances student-centered practices, this book instead utilizes critical research through affect theory to advance posthuman practices.

Another GroupMe

"Something that was challenging was getting students to show up to anything outside of class. I don't know why that was so hard, but it was hard . . . I promoted it on GroupMe," *it allows us to connect as peers . . . also I saw them in the [science] building between classes.*

The conversation continues. There was ambient music playing through the classroom speakers before this while the peer mentors were consuming the food in their Chick-fil-A boxes and lemonade. It unexpectedly starts up again, loudly, during a peer mentor's comment. She gets up to mute it. The conversation shifts. Another peer mentor notes:

It was better this year not having to hold office hours. Field trips were more difficult to schedule—GroupMe, then emails with students who wouldn't respond, then individual meetings.

Another: Has *been a peer mentor one on one before, it's harder in groups,* "they gang up. All of our communication has been over GroupMe; no one has attended meetings."

Another:

I do wish I had got to know them sooner, because now we talk a lot, especially before and after class, or when I see them in the [student union], or through the direct message function in GroupMe, I didn't even know that was there."? I don't know if you've thought about this, perhaps if the learning community class could be two days a week, and maybe the peer mentor could run one day, almost a study hall, or help them prep. I also helped many folks make their schedules.

Another:

It was hard being so much older than them. "I think it was our second meeting here that I learned what GroupMe is, that really helped a lot . . . It was hard to try to get anybody out of the classroom . . . we're doing our last event . . . next Tuesday, and nobody wants to commit to a date." It's been challenging to schedule with all the students' schedules. "I definitely had a good experience, it definitely helped me get involved a little bit more. I think what would have been better for me is if I had a chance at the beginning of class to really introduce myself . . . the teacher kind of did, but I think the way he introduced me gave me a really superior role, or above . . . not a peer. So it helped that a student I talked with . . . gave me credibility within the group . . . another thing I found challenging was really basic questions, like where buildings are on classes. I've taken 20 classes here and all but one have been in the same building . . ."

A chucklebuzz rumbles through the room. "I have all the resources [the learning community] provided me, but . . ." The chucklebuzz continues.

Involvement

An instructor lectures on the components of a theory, one of which is involvement. *Involvement. You're here, you'll never get this time back.* "You're in class, studying. You're not somewhere smoking pot and wasting your time." A buzz is sparked with the mention of pot. The instructor contin- ues. *Involvement—you don't have the time to commit crimes, be a criminal.*

No one takes notes. No fingers are on keyboards, no pencils or pens are pressed to paper. There is no notetaking, even in a class and a current moment full of definitions and lists. Two students are still stuck on the pot example. The sound of this side conversation dies out; the instructor's voice remains. A student writes something else on paper.

Terminology

Two full-time staff members who work with learning communities are currently out of the office. Other staff from the larger unit have been asked to fill in. To plan a faculty training. To keep the high-impact prac- tice momentum moving.

One of the staff members filling in reflects on an idea she had. "That was something I thought about last night. The enhancement experiences, which always sounds kind of sexual to me, I don't know." Another staff member replies, "Enrichment experiences. What's on *your* mind?"

Integrative Learning

Integrative learning, theorized as a component of deep learning and a high-impact practice, is measured at the student level by the NSSE by the following items:

> In your experience at your institution during the current school year, about how often have you done each of the following? Worked on a paper or project that required integrating ideas or information from various sources. Included diverse perspec- tives (different races, religions, genders, political beliefs, etc.) in class discussions or writing assignments. Put together ideas or concepts from different courses when completing assignments or during class. Discussed ideas from your readings or classes with faculty members outside of class. Discussed ideas from your readings or classes with others outside of class (students, family members, coworkers, etc.).[22]

Embedded in these items are a few presumptions, not the least of which being that integrative learning can be measured at the student level.[23] Measurement of integrative learning at the student level presumes a measurable atomization of integration, generally. If students are the unit of analysis here, it's easy to see how instructors are also a unit of analysis—say a question instead asking, "How often do you work with other instructors to put together ideas or concepts across courses when developing assignments or class activities?" This is indeed the frame that an atomized approach to integrative learning took at State U., and it's the frame its learning community instructors internalized. She asks an instructor to talk to her about integrative learning. The instructor begins with a values statement:

> For me, I want the class to be more about like how to maybe ask questions or know of things or learn about things right and then be able to just make that stepping stone so that they can go and do that eventually again. Right? Like if they go on to grad school program. They are like 'okay, wait, is there something similar?' They go on to a new job. And they're like, okay, how do I navigate this?' That's what I hope for more so, than just like . . .

The instructor pauses. Something changes. The frame flips from community values to an atomized responsibility. It isn't that the atomized responsibility shows the instructor not enacting their community values—it's more like the two levels are incommensurate:

> . . . anything else. I think in terms of doing it to others like the course relating to other classes, I don't know that it really particularly does. To put it point blank. I think I'm aware. Like, I know, particularly in the learning community I'm aware of what's going on in their [first linked] class. I'm aware of what's going on in their [second linked] class. I'm, you know, aware of what's going on in their [third quasi-linked] class and when assignments are due and x, y, z, but I mean . . . there was a day, the library day, the library scavenger hunt day. We did make those groups intentional based upon their groups for their [third] class's assignment to kind of get them more used to research together, that kind of thing. But that was the

only assignment that we were, you know, very much like: okay this is your group. So, I don't know that it directly relates to their classes.

Coordination

I'm "not privy to that information and well I mean I could probably be privy but I don't want to know."

They laugh together.

Desktops

Desktop objects have remained very similar across these first seven weeks. The same people who usually have laptops up have them up today. The person who scrolls through the McGraw-Hill-produced slides along with the instructor's lecture does so today. The person who takes notes in TextEdit with a rotation of consumer websites coming up from time to time does so today. The student who keeps his laptop screen in dark mode, obscuring what is visible at a distance to visual buzz, does so today. There are screens at the front of the room in front of the usual students that she can't see. The person who was sleeping during the class activity a few weeks ago is awake and has a big three-ring binder out. It's massive—at least two and a half inches thick. She takes notes of some kind on the left side of the binder, right-handed, dreads down, cowrie shells here and there. The student who never takes notes now has his head on his desk. The two students who like to have their books out with their notes have their books out with their notes. An ordinary day. An ordinary day?

Head on Desk Count

8:17 a.m. HODC: 0

8:30 a.m. HODC: 3

8:35 a.m. Hoodie up count: 7
Hat/beanie count: 5

Disruptions of Lecture Format

The classroom is set up in pods of three desks facing each other, with iMacs on each desk. Her seat today is in a pod at the front of the room. Her seat is in the front corner, in line with where the instructor is standing. She also faces toward the rest of the room instead of facing the instructor. She turns her chair toward the instructor and away from the desk. This location is disorienting.

This is an odd room layout for a lecture. There are lots of nooks and crannies. It's much more suitable for group work.

Most participation on this day comes from students sitting in the front half of the room. There is a large floor-to-ceiling beam in roughly the center of the room, side to side, and about two-thirds of the way to the back. There is a television attached to this beam that faces the lectern. The television alternates between showing the slides displayed on the projector at the front of the room and live camera shots of student areas in the room. The beam functions as a room divider.

A white male student sitting in the front of the room responds to another question from the instructor to the class. This student sits front and center in the room on the lectern side of the beam. This student is a demographic minority in the room: there are more Black students than white, and there are at least an equal number of women as men. And still he takes up space.

It's impossible to see what many students are doing and whether they have notes out or whether their eyes are open, what their facial expressions might be—most any hints about the level of their engagement—as the iMacs and the large beam and other students conspire to block most lines of sight.

Almost 100 percent of white students sit at pods of all-white students. Almost one hundred percent of students of color sit at pods with other students of color. Most students of color in this class are Black. There is one pod with two white students and one Black student.

The HVAC unit in this room is loud, and all sounds in this room echo. The academic advisor for students in this learning community is leading class today, and her voice echoes around the room. The echo of her voice is joined by the echo of the HVAC unit, as usual, even when she pauses her speech. She talks a bit louder than the regular instructor, so the volume of her voice with the echo is exponentially louder. There is now even more sound, as several students add to the cacophony by talking at once.

———

Another day.

Today the television attached to the beam in the center of the room is off. One less source of visual buzz. The projector is in use, as usual.

The sound of students flipping through printed-out lecture slides echoes around the room. Is this the sound of Engagement? Can it be disentangled from the HVAC noise?

Students have settled into their pods, in as much of a lecture format as this class allows, or, in the specific enactment of lecture format in this classroom. There are few questions asked between the instructor and students. Most students have their eyes open, but not all. At least that's her impression from behind an iMac, looking out to others behind their own iMacs.

———

Another day.

She sits at a different pod today, changing her orientation to the concrete pole situated at what is just about the center of the room. A visual and audio line to a different section of the room opens up, and some of her old pathways close down. The computer stations at each desk still block flows of sight, just differently. Sound emerges: the sound of typing, the metallic sound of an empty soda can hitting a desk. The instructor's voice rises above these, but his face is obscured from sight frequently, which makes it hard to read his lips and really understand what he is saying. The white noise from above—the sound of the HVAC—sinks down into all of the silos in the room created by pods of people and chairs and desks and iMacs, and a beam with a TV as well. Buzz flows. The classroom door opens to the outside of the building and it's propped, as it remains permanently locked. The sounds of the street adjacent to the classroom building seep in through the crack: a motorcycle roar, the smooth sound of a car moving displace the air around them.

Four students in her line of sight have laptops up in front of the iMacs on their desks. Two other students have notebooks out. Typing or writing in or on these devices is intermittent.

A student stretches back in their chair. Their chest and face are parallel to the ceiling for a brief moment, then they return to face a new slide in the front of the room. Slide changes prompt typing and writing. Typing posture snaps some students into straightening their backs, placing their arms to their sides, tilting their heads slightly downward to their monitor.

This video is four minutes and thirty-four seconds long. Most students' eyes are trained on the projector screen. Some students rotate to the direction of their desk, which for these students is not facing front. One student has their head in their hands, sitting up. This is a motion that's imperceptible to most of the room, given the setup of tables, iMacs, and the concrete pole. There are no notes being taken in this room, at least in so far as she can see or hear. Imperceptible.

Recruitment

At State U., recruitment for learning communities begins at orientation programming during June and July. Advisors for the communities weave a pitch for the communities into their presentations. The pitch contains a glossy video, elaboration on the benefits of participation for students, and an explanation of how learning communities work at State U.

She asks a learning community alumna about the process.

> Oh, I think it happened at my freshman orientation. My advisor . . . actually had did a presentation about it and me and me and my parents were just talking over it and just they were like, just go ahead and do it. Like at first, I didn't want to do it 'cause I was like, I don't know what this is. I like, like what is it going to do? Is it going to choose classes for me? Is it going to put me with the same people? Like I don't know. But then I actually just, you know, just signed up for it because I'm like "hey, this is something that could actually help me." But it took me a while. I had to read more about it before I just signed up.

Icebreaker

The room may be dark, but the peer mentor's eyes sparkle. She takes over running the class, breaking the twenty-four students into four groups of six. The room consists of seven tables with three chairs at each table. Students erupt into general chatter while the peer mentor stands at the front of the classroom, writing something into her notebook with a pen.

One representative from each group waits near the peer mentor for further instructions. She finally shows them what she wrote down, and after reading her notes they return to their groups. They clumsily act out parts of a sentence that are for their group mates to guess. They aren't allowed to communicate verbally.

One student texts on her phone, unperturbed by her surroundings.

The groups get rowdy, each student attempting to speak over the other with their guesses, hoping each new one might be the correct answer. More often than not, it is not. A group at the front left of the room works quietly, speaking in soft tones, piecing their secret sentence together.

Suddenly, someone yells, "Can we get a different person?" She is frustrated with the group leader, who is unable to communicate using words, and who is apparently not a great actor. Students across the room chuckle in response to her shout.

One student scrolls through Instagram on her phone, seemingly checked out.

Finally, the instructor calls time, bringing the class back together. The groups offer up their guesses at the correct answer. None of them guessed the complete sentence, but some came close. There are smiles among the students who collaborated peacefully together. For those who didn't, well . . . they don't appear to be making eye contact.

Engagement: 1. Community: 0.

Re/Defining Value

How do we come to value the student experience in learning communities? How might we be able to account for impact in excess of countable behaviors or actions?

Questions of value in higher education have ultimately redounded to the countable for decades if not far longer. To be accountable to outcomes requires this: everything else isn't enough. If we are "serious"[24] about providing students value, if we "owe it to students"[25] to make sure that their college education finishes quickly and results in a job, then to place any other formulation of values higher than metrics in the decisions that shape day-to-day practice would be grossly irresponsible. To value the useless would be malpractice.[26] The concept of high-impact practices rests on this very notion:[27] colleges and universities should provide high-impact practices for students because these are the environments that *count* the most. They count the most to metrics of student engagement, and student engagement counts the most toward metrics of on-time graduation. At State U., integrative learning is what makes learning communities *count* as a high-impact practice. When colleges think about what opportunities to offer students, it isn't just smart but responsible to offer high-impact practices first.

The determination of value through quantifiable impact exists in a time where the failures of metrics have accrued for decades. Colleges and universities need to look no further than to their own use of standardized testing in undergraduate and graduate admissions.[28] Similar features can be found across a generation of accountability to testing and value-added measurements in elementary and secondary education. Failures of metrics were evident in the gaming of metrics in the market crash of 2008.[29] Failures of metrics are also found in pop culture representations of this problem, such as the 2000s TV series *The Wire*,[30] frequently hailed as one of the best television shows of all time.[31] Its plot revolved around the problems that came to bear when the (fictional) Baltimore police were held accountable to metrics. We can even look to Robert McNamara's spectacular failure in Vietnam, where the business sense for metrics he brought to war planning devastated the Vietnamese as well as the American soldiers commanded to carry out orders linked to no value but an accounting.[32] This list is a snapshot. The failures of metrics applied to human behavior are the air we breathe, and yet these are the values one must hold to be a serious educator, administrator, and/or researcher in higher education. We must redefine value in higher education in order to be able to chart a different course forward for our students and our institutions.

This redefinition requires a continued refusal to impose structuring devices such as impact upon impasses. To value the impasse is to value ordinary, unquantifiable life within college and university communities. In our present moment, this is a revaluation of these communities beyond categorization, or metrics.[33] What would a mode of inquiry look like, say, a mode of inquiry about the value of learning communities, that refuses[34] impact? In one form, it might look like this book. To refuse impact, or other structuring devices such as student engagement or integrative learning, is not really to write up a bunch of anecdotes from learning communities and let them speak for themselves. That's not quite what we are up to here; although if read this way, this book hopefully still provides an in-depth *representation* of the inner workings of a learning community.

The refusal of impact at the core of this book takes two forms. First, it's the refusal to turn to a validating system to sort anecdotes into worthy or not worthy of inclusion here. Anecdotes are included here because they glowed for us. Glow is *pre-representational*, the quality of something that draws you in before you can express in words why.[35] Glow is subjective insofar as subjective is an effect of our social worlds, instead of another naming of individual. Second, it's the continued refusal to impose such a system upon the anecdotes that made it in. These anecdotes glow in excess of our authorial attachments to them. They glow in particular ways for you, the reader. After reading these anecdotes, they leave a residue that you can't quite categorize. That residue is glow. That glow is one form of the unquantifiable within learning communities. That glow gives a starting point to a revaluation of learning communities beyond categorization or metrics. Higher education is so thoroughly immersed in metricized values that it can be impossible to imagine any other system of values organizing our work. And yet, these values already exist in our universities.[36] The question of revaluing isn't one of creating new values from whole cloth, but rather attuning to the values beyond metrics that live in every moment all around us. This is the work to be done; this is the reading of this book that makes *a slightly restrained fever dream in service of the revaluation of classroom life* transformational.[37]

Revaluing higher education does not mean that the practices currently labeled *high-impact* should cease to exist so that newly valued practices may form. On the contrary—as high-impact practices by definition predated their naming as high impact, they all have histories of coming to value outside of this label. We live in a history wherein learning communities were valued differently. Revaluing higher education, and learning communities specifically, is less a practice of conjuring than it is attunement.

Applied Learning

There is a railroad track across their path. The instructor points to the track and tells the students, "Stand right there." One of the students exclaims, "Not on the track!" The instructor chuckles. He asks, "What's that concept? Obedience!"

The First Presentation

The group walks away, but before they get five steps from the podium the instructor asks the class if they have any questions for the presenters. A student asks a question, and the group gives a few sentences of good detail. One group member then quickly says, "Anyone else? No? Thank you!" and the group turns to leave. The class snickers.

The instructor raises his hand and says, "I do" and again stops them in their tracks. He asks a question and the group members take turns answering. The instructor asks again: "Any other questions?" This time, the group members aren't so quick to leave; they hang out in the impasse and wait for a hand. One group member tests their fate. "Darn, we were really hoping for another question," he says, while turning away—and a hand comes up.

Snickerbuzz.

A back-and-forth question-and-answer exchange happens with a student sitting in his usual seat, directly to the right of the pole in the center of the classroom that fractures the space of the room into pieces. He has to stand to be seen over the computers and TV blocking him and is still not visible to many people in class.

Another student at that pod—in front of the pole and television—asks another question. One group member takes the lead on this response, with his groupmate affirming his words after.

The instructor closes the impasse: "And thank you once more for volunteering to be the first presenters." Next week there will be more presentations. "And that's it, thanks all." Class was half over, but now class is completely over. It ends twenty-five minutes early.

Making Connections

One of the hallmarks of learning communities is the connection of course material across the linked courses.[38] There is planning that takes place among the leading faculty to intentionally connect course content (or at least there should be). But do the students feel like their learning community classes are connected beyond being linked? When asked about this at the end of the semester following the conclusion of her learning community, one student's response is,

> Yeah, so that's actually really funny because I was talking to my literature teacher about it. I had gotten a really good rela-

tionship with her, but I was starting to say like when I seen the curriculum . . . for a [field of study] major, I was like, "What does English literature have to do with anything as far as [field of study]?" But it's like you get in these classes and you start to see, well in [field of study], you have to learn how a person thinks or you have to learn how to communicate with someone, you have to learn how to read in between the lines. So, it's like, that's what literature is about. Literature is all about studying what someone says to you or studying the tone of something or a person's body language just studying somebody beyond the simple thing that they have to say. So it's like, I was starting to see that in all of my classes and it just, it was really crazy because when I first started, I was like, it really makes no sense to be in all of these . . . classes, but it's like as you go along you start to learn. Like, for example, I also took a[n] acting class when I was like at why, why would acting be on a curriculum for [field of study]? But when I was in my acting class, he was starting to teach us how our brain connects with our body and our mind and how our body tells us to do certain things when it comes to moving and talking. And it's just like, wow, I would have never thought that a[n] acting class would relate to a [field of study] class when it really does. So, I definitely see it in all of my classes now. I see how it all comes back to [field of study].

Involvement

"The one last thing I want to talk with you about today is" our involvement assignment. She projects a Google Doc with the assignment details. Research shows involvement is good, "but I'm not going to bore you with the statistics. I'm gonna make you become the statistic."

Library Day

Students are scattered around seven round tables in a windowless library classroom. The friendly librarian instructor for the day splits the class into seven groups, based on where they are seated. No purposeful mixing of strangers on this day! The librarian explains that each group is tasked with completing ten missions, and she hands them computer tablets that contain further instructions.

"This is not meant to be a competitive exercise."

Famous last words?

As if surrounded by family, students leave their backpacks on the floor and on the chairs in the room before leaving for their mission. They file out of the room to begin their scavenger hunt.

Three of the teams remain behind. It appears that the missions are in a different order for each group. The students are huddled around computers, speaking quietly to each other and looking up information.

On the screen in the middle of the room there is an activity feed with pictures from each team that has submitted the answers to one of their missions. The mathematics tutoring center. A book. A selfie of a smiling group in front of the bagel shop. They appear to be successful, and they appear to be having fun.

The group of four students at the far side of the room is speaking to the peer mentor about housing issues. Ostensibly, this isn't related to one of their missions, but they are using resources of a kind. The peer mentor advocates for the role of resident assistants, saying RAs have a lot of responsibilities and may not be able to immediately turn their attention to a particular concern. She can't hear the students' response, but their faces reflect apt attention.

Thirty minutes after they departed, three of the groups return to the classroom with their ten missions complete. There are no prizes for being the first to return. The librarian meant it when she said this wasn't a competition. The students sit back down at their original tables. Some of them are on their phones; others are speaking quietly with each other. The screen in the front of the room still shows a waterfall of pictures and answers from the remaining groups.

A fourth group of students returns. One of the students in that group complains to the librarian about how "unfairly difficult" their assigned book was to find. The librarian confirms that some of the books are more challenging to locate.

There are still groups missing, but in the interest of time the librarian begins to go over the answers to the scavenger hunt. One student is on his phone. The rest appear to be listening. He may be listening, too. It's hard to determine.

"Are there any questions?" the librarian asks, wrapping up the class. A student asks about the elevator in the building. It's an old elevator, but it works well enough to transport students to the different levels of stacks.

The final groups return from their missions just as class is dismissed. The peer mentor mentions offering a study session for one of their other learning community classes. In the general shuffle and rumble of packing up and leaving she misses the response of the students. Or maybe that is the response.

The Inescapable Ontogenetic Force of Inquiry

To value the useless in higher education is to dislodge value from static concepts like earnings-potential-by-declared-major and time-to-degree and develop new questions of value that radiate from each other without end.[39] When the value of higher education is in the useless, measurements of value are not just undesirable, but non-sense.

Practices of research-creation take seriously the inescapable ontogenetic force of research. Ontogenetic? Here, we mean this quite literally. Research creates realities. Research-creation is a practice of values creation and worldmaking. In other words, research-creation honors the notion that our everyday acts of inquiry create realities. Research-creation is an artful practice in the sense that it describes a way of thinking-being and neither a person (an artist) nor an object.[40] As such, research-creation in higher education is available to all actors and involves a radical commitment to experimentation. It is neither side of a theory-practice binary: it is a practice that transcends boundaries of researcher, practitioner, and administrator. It does not seek to categorize and thus negate. Research-creation is a practice of affirmation.

Affirmation is an experimentation without hypothesis and without preset conditions. Affirmation does not predict, it acts. Research-creation as affirmation does not negate practice through an emphasis on theory and does not negate theory through an emphasis on practice: it does not negate—it affirms. In this affirmation, research-creation "does not see negation as its other. It operates in a completely different logic. Affirmation creates the trajectory, and from there the potential of the what else emerges."[41] A theory-practice binary operates on negation, that is, practice is not theory, and theory is not practice. Research that emphasizes its use to either side of this binary does so with an implicit *not the other side* attached. Affirmation asks the inquisitive[42] instead to simply experiment, and in doing so, create.[43] Research in the theory-practice binary produces new worlds within this binary. Research-creation produces new worlds, and thus re/values.[44] Research-creation is a practice of the ordinary, the infrathin, the not-yet, the useless, the impasse. Anecdotes are necessarily imperfect representations of this ordinary practice.[45] Research-creation creates worlds in excess of the valuations that create our current dystopia wherein higher education is being vultured by capitalist administrators, vendors, policymakers, foundations, agenda-setting organizations, students, and faculty—and in which critics too act as vulture capitalists in supporting the very actions they (we) denounce.[46]

What Is Student Engagement?

A learning community student is talking about his involvement in a student club that relates to his major—and the theme of his learning community. His face lights up when he talks about it, and his speech quickens. His learning community experience was only a semester long, and it seems like this student group has informally provided a community structure for him and, to his telling, several of his former learning community classmates. He

> first heard about it that first class . . . that was that first Monday we were ever there. I got a couple emails about it before, just general [field of study] emails about it. But that was really the first like true promotion that I got it was more of a just sorta kinda a bigger push, I would say, you know, they handed out flyers and stuff like that. I found it, you know, really useful just to talk to someone about it because I wasn't really sure what it was. And since I am I know an officer in that group. So, just looking at our engagement numbers. We don't have too many freshmen, we really, really don't have too many freshmen and that's something I've been trying to fix. To be completely honest, I've been trying to get more underclassmen involved.

Now her face lights up. *Engagement, you say? Engagement numbers?* A spark! Her speech quickens, her attention deviating from the list of questions she has to ask to this spark. She elaborates on her interest in engagement: it's somewhere between illuminating and rambling. The spark is all light and no heat. She gets to the point: "What do you mean when you think when you're talking about the engagement of freshmen and your student group like is that just attendance or is it something kind of . . ."

> . . . I really think it's more than attendance. I think it's contin-
> ued growth . . . outside of your classes. So, you know, coming
> to club meetings and learning more that you might not hear
> in your classes. Coming to, you know, develop your résumé.
> It's doing things you wouldn't necessarily do in class and that
> you're actively seeking out so we want those people to be a
> actively seeking opportunities and we will give them tools to
> actively seek out those opportunities.

What is student engagement? That which exceeds the formal curriculum and requires students to act outside of format.

Their discussion comes back to the idea of student engagement, this time in relation to the formal curriculum, his assigned learning community courses. She wants to know to what degree his participation in a learning community made him feel engaged at the university. This sparks him once more, and he gives an even longer exposition:

> I felt a lot of engagement, just because of the way that the pro-
> fessors sorta kinda knew it was [a learning community]. They
> knew we were together so they would just see we're kind of,
> you know, aware of the fact that we're together so, you know,
> they made sure to point that out, you know, they're like, you
> know, use your resources, you know, you know, if you have
> a partner for this, you guys can go library. It's just kind of
> introducing to some of those resources. I feel as a freshman,
> it was better just because of the way they introduced some
> of the resources to us. Like, you know, the library just sorta
> kinda doing some other stuff with that. You know, our . . . peer
> mentors, the tutoring center student support services, you know,
> we had our first-year advisor . . . come in a couple times she
> introduced herself for the people that didn't get to meet her at
> [orientation]. So, it was just sorta kinda seeing all that stuff just
> together. Just sorta kinda introducing to the ins and outs of like
> the bureaucratic stuff that wouldn't necessarily be introduced,
> you know, talking to people who I know who aren't in any

forms of [learning communities] they're sorta kinda lost when it comes to some of this bureaucratic stuff. They don't know who their advisor is. They didn't know they were supposed to meet with their advisor and they don't even know, like, you know, your professors are supposed to be there for you. They aren't supposed, you're supposed to, you know, like fight them like that's not what you're supposed to do. You're supposed to, you know, there's a hierarchy to it, you know, you go the department head and, you know, you do all that stuff. And I thought, you know, personally just, you know, because of the [learning community] it made me more likely, I actually met with my advisor, more than like I meet with her more than once a semester. I meet with her multiple times a semester because, you know, we have the in-person things. She's like, "I'm here for you, like, whatever you need. You can come to me, like . . . I'm here for you."

His picture of student engagement shifts. Student engagement becomes a technology, that which extends the formal curriculum or suggests students act outside of format. What is student Engagement? It must be all of these things, at least in this moment, in these hauntings, for this student.

Why Did Y'all Show?

After class, she sticks around. Everyone else sticks around—their main learning community classes are scheduled back to back in the same room. One hour and fifteen minutes of class, a fifteen-minute break, and then another one hour and fifteen minutes of class. She only attends the first one. Class ended early today, so there is now a thirty-two-minute break between classes. A student notes this out loud to the class. It also seems that the second class is not, in practice, one hour and fifteen minutes at all. One student has kept records. He says the average run time for the next class is twenty-two minutes, and there was one class period that had a negative run time. According to his records, class both started and ended before it was scheduled to begin. Another student decides not to stick around for the next class. He leaves us to walk to the math tutoring center to see if they are offering algebra tutoring right now. He tells her he is "about to fail that class." Another student in the front of the room asks her if she came to class yesterday. She says no—the instructor mentioned that there would be no class last week after many folks had already left the room. It seems that several students in the class showed up; they think, *He really needs to communicate better.* The student leaving for math tutoring didn't get the memo, and on his way out now complains that he could've gone to the gym at that time.

Someone asks her what she thought about class today. She simply says, "the usu." Someone else says that what was notable was that no one was there. She revises her remarks to the group; those were her thoughts exactly. She asks the question on her mind. To her, *what was notable right now was not why did others not show up, but why did y'all show?* Answers vary: *I paid for this class, I would feel guilty, I wouldn't be doing anything else in my room, it's a waste not to show up, I don't want the instructor to feel bad.* The Black students in the room keep mostly to themselves during this discussion. They sit on the left side of the room, not physically integrated into the hub of activity. Two are on their phones. One of these students is still working with his phone and laptop combination that he was Engaged with during class. The students in this class are STEM majors, and about half appear to her to be Black—and notwithstanding this simple count of equity, the white students take up a lot of space in this discussion and in general. She usually lets the class conversation flow around her, but this time she asks a question, and she wants to give the body language that the question is for all, not just the (mostly white) talkative right side of the room. A Black student turns to her and says in a low voice that *it's a waste to not show up to classes, and to have classes run so short.* She agrees.

For all of the many conceptions of waste that exist, this seems to fit most. Is it a waste of Engagement? What would that look like? Surely it's something more than shortening class time. Is it a waste to Engage in a class with an aggressive lecture format? An aggressive format of any type? Is Engagement a function of movement, surprise, being on your toes and in the moment because you aren't sure what is next? That's a definition that isn't so much dependent on having the correct format but on breaking whatever the dominant format might be. Active learning could itself be a format. By this definition, engagement would flow not from the enactment of a proper format, but in the play between formats.[47]

Frequent, Timely, and Constructive Feedback I

It is a cool day in December and the last day of class for this learning community course. In this course, that means the last day of class rituals. The instructor opens the class with a few of them.

He wants students to feel free to continue to reach out to him, even after the end of the term: "If you need my help with anything, send me an email, come to my office. I like to establish long-term relationships with my students. We are building life-long relationships. My job is to help you succeed . . . send me an email, I'll find the time for you." The instructor comes back to this point a few minutes later: "One thing people in this class can't say is [instructor] doesn't respond to email. I respond to everything. I respond to everything . . . I'm not just here for a paycheck, I'm here to help you succeed."

The instructor lets students know about the two summer 2020 classes he is teaching. Each is online, and he will create an environment like an in-person class. It wasn't a thought in anyone's mind at this point that this specification will become unnecessary; every single State U. summer course moved online in 2020.

The instructor then discusses student evaluations. *The evaluation system is open, so please take them. Any criticism just helps make class better.*

The instructor then begins the lecture. This too is a class ritual, though not specific to the last day. No notes walks into class late, the instructor has to open the door to let them in, and they move to take their seat, no backpack on them and nothing in their hands. Another class ritual.

It's a little over twenty minutes before class is scheduled to end, but the instructor is moving to end class. They haven't said it yet, but you can feel it. A few rituals proceed at once. The instructor stands in front of the room and begins to say goodbye: "I wish you all well, I wish you all success." A student in front of her whispers to another student: "Should we clap?" No one claps. At this same moment, the instructor concludes: "Alright, thank you guys." No notes begins a round of applause. It's a loud round of applause, and from her view, the whole class has joined in. Applausebuzz. A student asks if they could all take a class picture. She steps in to take the picture so that everyone in class can be in frame. They say a class concept together instead of *cheese*. And with that, folks go their own way.

One student says on their way out: "Honestly, *this instructor* is the most important one to take a picture with."

Chapter Five

Impasse (2020–21)

Dies Iræ, Dies Illa, Buzz

What has become of buzz in pandemic life? Certainly, there continue to be matters to attend to in our lives that do not quite rise to the level of clear words and phrases or discernible discourse. The sociotechnical apparatus of Zoom, with these particular students and instructors, in these particular pandemic times, and at this particular university, mediates buzz in particular ways. Buzz, as it lived before, has died. Long live buzz.

To say that buzz, this nascent structuring device of our own, has died is laden with irony. Can we think through a judgment day of buzz? A day on which it died and an organizing power decided its fate? What is the requiem for buzz? What is buzz's "dies iræ, dies illa / day of wrath and doom impending"?[1] The day that State U. shut down in-person operations and went remote in March 2020 might be one such day. But things were never that clear. State U. had fully online classes and programs before the pandemic that continued on course in pandemic times. Was there never buzz in these? In fact, classes that moved online aren't even themselves devoid of in-person community, particularly for the one learning community we are observing this year that is indeed a residential learning community. It's ordinary in these classes to see a student in one Zoom tile along with their roommate in the background and then see the reverse of this image in another Zoom tile: the roommate logged into Zoom front and center, and the original student now visible in the background. These students very much had an in-person classroom experience, just very differently mediated. And what about students with roommates in different classes? What about students with no roommates? What about students living off campus with family and friends, or on their own? When we wrote of buzz in prepandemic times, we wrote not simply of imperceptible incursions of other human voices but also of the buzz of HVAC systems filling rooms. Certainly, HVAC systems didn't die with the pandemic. In fact, they gained a particular importance. While we claimed buzz was *in its first instance a sonic experience* we also wrote of visual buzz, and we defined buzz as an affect broadly. Sighted students certainly still experience visual buzz in Zoomland, even if simply the moments when screenshares foul up a previous visual stasis or Internet connectivity issues cause video connections to come and go. So perhaps it's premature to hold a requiem for buzz. Did buzz ever die? Did buzz ever live?

The buzz we are experiencing in in-person learning community classrooms is barely comparable to the buzz (if it existed at all) in emergency remote online learning communities. However, its precondition, *the presumed still and silent state of all persons but one in a space that allows buzz to become tangible*, is present in spades. Buzz itself, a sense at the threshold of perceptibility, mostly fades into the *still and silent state* of Zoom classrooms. A different but still thoroughly present lecture format persists, and within this format, buzz is mostly imperceptible. It's ordinary to not see students in human form at all when instructors don't require cameras on: and sometimes, even when they do. A camera on doesn't mean a face in view; it often meant a partial face and a healthy portion of a ceiling. It's ordinary not to hear the background noise of the classroom if we consider a classroom to be constituted by the full collection of students and faculty in a shared physical environment. The sounds of classmates and their environments in Zoomland must enter the classroom through microphones, and Zoom etiquette typically requires all microphones to be muted except the speaker. When microphones are muted, there is no opportunity for a collective classroom sonic buzz experience as there is in-person. The case that Zoom etiquette seeks to avoid, multiple microphones on and multiple users speaking, is a sonic buzz particular to the sociotechnical apparatus of Zoom. When this form of sonic buzz happens, the cacophony is mediated, the green light encircling speakers flips back and forth, sometimes the audio mixes, and sometimes it too flips back and forth. In many instances, though, all microphones but one are muted. Classrooms have sunk into lecture format in a sociotechnical system that reinforces the *still and silent state of all persons but one in a space.* If this is the new normal, it feels a whole lot like the old normal: it just wears pajama bottoms instead of pants. For the most part, buzz became imperceptible.

Buzz *became* different in emergency remote learning. Buzz *is* different in fully online courses and programs. Visual buzz is camera shots of foreheads with ceilings. Sonic buzz is the strange sounds that made it through the shared audio channel, most certainly mixed with the barely perceptible sounds from where we each Zoom in, inaudible to others with our microphones muted but certainly part of our own classroom experience. Experience has fractured; buzz has fractured. Buzz is a product of the sociotechnical apparatus of its space and time. Buzz hasn't quite individualized, as the classroom itself hasn't individualized. Buzz is a shared experience, differently. Buzz is different.

Thursday Slump

As the semester progresses, the experience of attending classes on Zoom day in and day out appears to take its toll on the students. Over time, more students are absent from class, and those present are by all appearances disengaged. This week, the students have a guest speaker discussing how to write résumés. The Thursday afternoon slump is very evident this week. Several students yawn, and there are more students lying in bed than usual. As the guest speaker continues sharing, the students' eyes aren't directed toward the camera. They appear to look away from the camera screen at some object not visible to her, but maybe they aren't looking at anything specific as they simply disengage. The instructor has already told her that chat messages have been sent to individual students who are lying in bed, falling asleep, or engaging in behaviors that appear to indicate that they are inattentive. *How many private chat messages are being sent today?* One student appears to fall asleep. The guest speaker ends the presentation and asks the students if they have any questions. There is no response from the students. After the guest logs off the Zoom session, the instructor asks the students to describe the relevance of the content of today's class. One of the students who regularly answers the instructor's questions unmutes and shares some thoughts. She wonders if the instructor feels a sense of gratefulness for this student's willingness to end awkward silences and speak up in class.

Parameters

The instructor dismisses students one by one once they let him know in what city they currently reside. Finally, it's just the instructor and two of the authors in the Zoom room. The instructor explains he didn't want to teach the course synchronously, but his departmental advisor talked him into it. He asks, "You think it came across that I don't help with technical issues?"

After-Class Email

"By the way y'all, I get a saved file of Zoom chat after the meeting ends 😵‍💫."

Ennui, Part II

Each day is the same. The students are the same, their cameras on or off, their faces displayed or maybe their beds, their ceilings, their bare walls. The instructor is the same, lecturing from shared slides without looking at the chat or at students' faces. His voice is steadily droning on about the subject at hand, lacking inflections that would break up the monotone. The chat box is also the same. It's empty, as always. It has been disabled by the instructor to prevent students from misbehaving. She struggles to stay awake enough to do her work. Two large mugs of coffee don't seem to suffice to make this drudgery less of a drudge at 8 a.m. two days each week.

In the same class two days later, she observes more of the same.

In Retrospect, in Memoriam

One of the workshop facilitators had taught as part of a learning community before, two years prior. Her workshop was aimed at transfer students who enrolled in four courses together. She ended up with a group of fourteen students. The learning community's big question was related to social media. The students' culminating experience was an e-portfolio and a poster presentation of original research.

This type of learning community was an outlier at her institution where most learning communities were retention tools for first-year students. They were high-impact practices, if you will. Original research, a virtual showcase, and a poster were well beyond some of the other faculty's goals for their learning communities. But the workshop facilitator emphasizes the rapport between students and their retention had made the learning community worthwhile.

A one-time learning community for that particular instructor. Anecdotal evidence of warm fuzzies.

Fun and Games

"You are all a community. You are all on the same path." The instructor smiles and introduces herself in an upbeat, conversational tone. She shares her screen and reviews the course syllabus. "This class is to help you." She discusses Zoom etiquette and how to handle technical difficulties, emphasizing that she wants "this to be a fun experience." Whether she means this class, this learning community, or this semester is unclear.

She adds, "If you have any questions, I am happy to help you."

The peer mentor, too, seems eager to help students. "Somebody please talk to me, ask me a question, or share about themselves because I am sure everyone has similar questions or concerns." One by one, several students unmute themselves and ask about success strategies for online courses, study tips for the asynchronous course, and the impact of the COVID-19 pandemic on the practical aspects of their major. The peer mentor provides some specific recommendations for organization. She encourages students to write down due dates. "Plan out your schedule and stay organized." She shares strategies for time management and urges students to take advantage of their resources. The instructor chimes in about the learning community's asynchronous course, explaining contact hours and homework hours and how much time students can expect to spend on each.

The class concludes with structured introductions, first modeled by the instructor and then the peer mentor. Students verbally introduce themselves. Once introductions are complete, the instructor dismisses class early. But only this once.

Integration

Integration was an issue in several learning communities observed last year, and the office that trains learning community faculty makes this a focus of faculty training for the next year. For this office, following the literature, integration of learning community courses is an integral part of what makes them high-impact. Training begins with a prompt for faculty to define what integration means to them. Take about five to ten minutes, write it out on your own, drop it into the Zoom chat when ready. Mics stay muted. There are 48 participants in this Zoom meeting, and 24 of 48 cameras are now off. One camera that's on has no human in view. Where videos are on and humans are in view, the writing or typing it looks like folks are doing seems like an indicator that they are thoughtfully engaged in the training, although it could be anything. Seven minutes after the original prompt is given, the responses roll into the chat, one after another:

Faculty 1: "Tech integration. I think I began integrating tech into my classroom teaching in 2008, as a GTA."

Faculty 2: "For me, one way of integration is a transdisciplinary approach to the tackling of (wicked) problems, requiring and training scientific, personal, social, and technical skills."

Trainer 1: "Tech integration is a good example, [faculty 1]. What is some tech and how is it 'integrated' vs added on."

Faculty 3:

> What is integration? This is giving the students the opportunity to take a deep dive into their subject of interest. It strengthens the community bonds of learning between the class and faculty and gives the students a sense of belonging and gives their instructor a chance to get to know them outside of the strictures of class where there is always the academic pressure of the next exam. An example: I remember hearing about a group of friends in a class that started with the project of refurbishing a broken-down vintage car. They started simply in their out-of-class time in understanding how it worked and eventually did a GoFundMe and drove cross country while updating their followers on social media. I cannot find the link for it now but it bonded them together and was a fantastic learning experience.

The responses continue to roll in, their volume overwhelms any ability to take collective stock of them in the moment. Responses pepper the chat, further complicating things. Some faculty give the definition of integration they think is best applicable to the topic of learning communities: "Integration for learning community is when two or more courses overlap in theme and/or content and show both similarities and differences across the disciplinary approaches to the same or similar problems so students can achieve a better, more in-depth understanding of the material." Many others give definitions of integration in terms of their home discipline, from citing philosophers to examples involving rock climbing. There is a trend also in describing integration as facilitating "a common goal," or "the collective effort and collaboration of mutual and diverse ideas, values and purposes in order to meet goal(s)," or the "bringing together and uniting of things"—integration as the creation of a master narrative or structuring device. There is a master narrative of integration itself that this section of training is designed to gather folks toward, and, the chat speaks back to this. The chat is a collection of sparks and splinters of the master narrative. Without the ability to make a cohesive whole out of integration in the chat (the program that continues through audio and video does this), her eyes are drawn to a collection of definitions that define integration as a paradox:

Faculty 4: "Integration is a process of recognizing that different perspectives can speak to one another in consensual yet also disjunctive ways. Integration is not hybridity and it is not seamlessness. Integration is creating a space where conflicting perspectives are used to form multi-faceted and layered forms of knowledge. Integration in HE asks students to consider how contradictory and at times clashing ideas inform how they make sense of the world"

Faculty 5: "I was thinking that integration is like a zipper. It involves interlacing two (or more) different ideas, concepts, subjects, etc. together. Importantly, the components should reveal something greater about themselves than the mere sum of their individual parts."

Faculty 6: "Integration means to bring things together, like puzzle pieces. They are fine on their own, but together paint a bigger picture. In education it can be used to bring two worlds together, facilitating enduring understanding. An example of this is when we learn songs to remember parts of the skeleton or all of the states. It can make a difficult task fun."

Teaching Assistant

The class is introduced to Cody the cat on the very first day. He's fifteen years old and the instructor got him from the shelter at twenty-one pounds. Most days, the class is let into the Zoom room right on time. When the video connects, they can see Cody, usually perched on the couch directly behind the instructor. Cody sleeps through class, mostly.

. . .

One day, the instructor admits class two minutes early. Two-thirds of students are already present. The instructor shares his screen. Today's topic is chapter 3. The instructor is wearing a headset. Cody the cat isn't on the couch.

. . .

The next class period they are admitted from the waiting room one minute prior to class. Most of the students are present. The instructor is sitting on the couch, his cat behind him.

. . .

They're 45 minutes into a 75-minute class period. The instructor resumes his screen share to continue today's topic of class discussion. One student is still taking notes. Her room is well-lit. Another student is unmuted, perhaps accidentally so. The instructor asks for everyone to mute themselves, saying "I'm getting some background noise, aside from my cat snoring. There's something else going on." The student mutes herself.

. . .

Another morning, the same Zoom room. The instructor sits down on the couch. Cody the cat jumps up behind him. Despite his twenty-one-pound weight he appears to be an agile cat. The instructor is wearing a headset. He locks the Zoom room and starts class by calling out students whose Zoom tiles are either too dark or their camera is pointed at the ceiling. He moves on to explain the format of the quiz this week. Cody settles in for the day.

. . .

It's midway through the term. As usual, the class is admitted to the Zoom room a few minutes prior to the start time. Today about half of the students are present. One person is in bed. They yawn and stretch; their eyes are open, and they are perhaps ready for class.

The instructor's camera is focused on Cody the cat. A few student cameras are still turned off, but class hasn't started yet.

. . .

Two days later, class is slow to start. It's one minute after start time and there are few students here. The instructor turns to Cody and asks, "Alright, are you ready for this, buddy?" He pets the cat. It's two minutes into class and the instructor locks the Zoom room.

. . .

It's one minute prior to the start of class. Everyone is muted. The instructor tries and tries to get Cody to jump up on the back of the couch. The cat doesn't seem interested in acting as his teaching assistant today.

Midway through class, the instructor interrupts his lecture, saying, "Sorry you guys, I'm going to have to spray some spray. Cody just bombed us. Cody is having some gastro issues." One student grins, but she tries to hide it with her hand. Another student is sitting in a desk chair with a rounded back. She has her phone in her left hand and is scrolling. It appears she missed the instructor's remark.

. . .

Several students have been logging off or were booted from class by the instructor. One camera displays a bed with a padded headboard and stacked-up pillows. If there is a student in this bed, then they are obscured by the name on their tile.

A notification dings, indicating that another student leaves the Zoom room. The instructor has been lecturing from the exam review nonstop for about twenty-five minutes. Another student leaves. The lecture stops abruptly. "Sorry, my cat just farted. Okay, chapter 4, new topic."

A student sits up, fixes her hair, and leans back. Another student leaves. They're down to two-thirds of the class.

. . .

They are let into the Zoom room three minutes prior to class. The instructor is petting his cat. He puts on his headset with microphone and looks at something on his cellphone. A bell dings every time new participants arrive. Cody tries to get up and leave and the instructor tries to get him to stay. The instructor smiles.

The instructor locks the Zoom room and says, "Good morning." He explains he had thought about postponing this class, but as chapter 10 is really long he wants to get started on it. The class midterm is coming up. It is 25 percent of the class grade, and the instructor encourages students to give it the attention it deserves. "This will be a short class so we can go back to sleep. Or, for some of you, continue sleeping."

. . .

Despite the instructor's email to the class yesterday about sleeping students, there are students still in bed. Several of them, in fact. Cody is cleaning himself on the couch behind the instructor.

. . .

The instructor concludes class. *Here we are moving into the weekend again. Tuesday we'll finish up this chapter and we'll talk about [new topic]. Cody may have chewed a cable. Please be working on your article reviews. I will see you all on Tuesday. Have a good weekend.*

. . .

"Get out of there!! My cat is just eating stuff in the corner, I don't even know what it is."

COVID

A student indicates that their parent is concerned about the spike in COVID-19 cases. The student's parent may not want the student to return to campus, and the student has two in-person classes. The instructor asks if there are other students who are in the same situation. One student raises their hand, and another student unmutes and indicates their parents feel the same. The instructor indicates that she currently doesn't have any information but will find out what she can for students and post it in Blackboard.

The Chat Box

The instructor, the peer mentor, and the graduate assistant discussed some changes in student behaviors on Zoom from the previous session. The instructor said, "Last week I would have given them a D or a F, this week I'll give them a C+." The instructor continues, saying, "I kicked one student out of the [Zoom session] because the student was falling asleep." The instructor also indicated the regular use of the private chat feature, sending some students direct messages to remind the student to sit up, be visible in the camera, and to pay attention. "I prefer to send them a private message rather than 'call them out' in class."

DisEngagement

For faculty used to the face-to-face classroom environment, student Engagement in emergency remote instruction can be difficult to assess.

The course content is presented in mostly lecture format with few instructor-student or student-student interactions. It's the limits of technology rather than effort that creates a feeling of disconnection as distractions in students' physical environments may hinder their attention. She notes that it's hard to determine in Zoom, but the students don't appear to be focused on the information being provided in class on this day. There are six students lying in bed with five only partially visible on screen and two with their eyes closed. She also notes that there is one student who has their camera on but is nowhere in sight. There are five students who appear to be sitting up, but they are only partially visible on camera. As the class session continues, more students become only partially visible on camera as the monotony sets in. The distractions become too much to ignore for some of the students as two of them are speaking with someone off camera in their physical space, laughing, smiling, talking while muted. How will the monotony and distractions impact their performance on the upcoming assignment? How will it affect their performance in the course?

Another Perspective

The peer mentors try to provide guidance and support for the students in the one-credit advisory course. They discuss their perception of the students' transition to college while simultaneously adjusting to synchronous online courses. One peer mentor shares that many of the students said that it was an adjustment for them to be online and that, for many, it was even harder because a lot of their classes were asynchronous. Many of the students the peer mentor supported said they struggled with personal motivation, stating that they didn't want to get out of bed to attend class. Some students also reported that their classes were hard or they struggled with making time to study because many of the students had teachers in high school reminding them to study and complete their homework. These challenges, coupled with the unique expectations of self-directed, asynchronous courses made it even more difficult for many of the first-semester students to feel successful in their college courses during the COVID-19 pandemic.

Routine

She has begun to establish a routine for observing the one-credit classes. Once the class is started by the instructor, she notes the time and counts the number students present, how many have their cameras on, and how many faces are visible to the rest of the class. She counts blankets, ceiling fans, and students who are lying down. She feels like the notes should describe something profound about the students, but her notes often reflect what the instructor or the guest speaker is sharing rather than what the students are saying or doing. Students are often muted and even when they appear to be engaged—that is, they're sitting up and facing the camera—many opportunities provided to engage verbally with the instructor, the guest speaker, or other students are met with silence. It feels awkward. Sometimes two or more students will unmute and start talking at the same time. No one knows which student should go first, so they mute their microphones again and stay silent. Over time, the effort to unmute to interject seems too much to attempt, and it's easier to sit in silence. When the class slides into this Zoom lecture format while the instructor or guest speaker lectures, she turns her attention from the students and takes note of the information that's presented that captures her attention. An available program she didn't know existed or a service that's provided that will be helpful for students to use become the focus of her notes. At least she's learning something new, and she hopes the students are, too, even if the students' behaviors don't clearly point to their engagement in the class.

Lightbulb Moment

There are several administrators and/or faculty fitfully designing a series of learning community faculty workshops. Angst permeates the space for multiple reasons. Two other administrators are on leave, creating a vacuum of leadership and institutional knowledge. There has been unclear or mixed communication about the roles and levels of involvement of the seven educators. The workshop has been moved to a virtual space. Four folks in this Zoom room have no experience with delivering online trainings. Two of the administrators are working from home amid their young children. One printer is almost out of ink, and there is zero budget for office supplies right now.

Later, one of the facilitators provides some context about a meeting prior to this one. She explains her confusion with the situation: "And it takes a while to kind of figure out what the problem is, like, you know, they've done workshops in the past, you know, there are these spreadsheets or worksheets. And so, after a while we're pushing, like, what's the goal? Why, why all this angst about this workshop? And it turns out that the past learning communities had really low integration between courses. And that was the moment we went 'ohh!' "

Distractions

Learning like this with no interaction is such a challenge. Fifty-four minutes have passed with no stopping of the screen share yet today. It's also early in the day, and there is a distinct lack of buzz, a lack of bouncing energy and ideas off other students and the instructor in the classroom. The classroom is this time/space void. It's not a "real" class.

The bed is ever the temptation. She silently applauds the students who are sitting up, at desks or tables. Yet she is unsure if any of them are even taking notes. (Not that note taking is *the* conclusive signal of engagement.) And always looming is that smartphone with its incoming texts and Instagram and Twitter feeds (she, too, is guilty of succumbing to their lure). No activity in the chat, as usual.

In one Zoom tile, a student is sitting up, but she's busy, moving around. She cleans her ear with a Q-tip and looks at what she dug up. The normalization of bringing noneducational activities such as cleaning one's ears and sleeping naked in a bed to a classroom where they would otherwise be out of the ordinary is stupefying.

The instructor asks: "Do you remember what Smith's theory was?" Silence. "Nobody?"

Nobody.

Virtual Cocurriculum

The instructor explains he'll be working from home and not be going to campus this semester. As a result, students are encouraged to reach out and schedule appointments to be conducted via Zoom or by phone. The instructor adds that there will be no face-to-face extracurricular events this semester, as was common in previous iterations of this learning community. There will, however, be a virtual movie screening. "Just kinda living day by day here, trying to make this learning community as fun as possible. First time teaching online with so many students. We'll all try our best."

Juvenile Education

For many of the students and all of the instructors, their homes now double as classrooms and job sites. The lines between personal space and professional space are blurred; in fact, in many cases these boundaries are almost nonexistent. Some students and instructors attempt to emulate the classroom environment by sitting at desks with the door to their room closed and minimal background activity, while others sit, or even lie, on beds, couches, or other comfortable furniture. Faces appear in the background, passing through, asking questions. Most are somewhat fleeting; some linger and muted conversations ensue. Sometimes cameras are turned off for the duration of the background activity. Other times, the activity continues visible to all in attendance.

Today's class topic focuses on volunteerism. As she scans the tiles, some show students' faces, some do not.

1:42 p.m. She settles on a tile with a student sitting on a couch. A child sits on the other side of the student.

The lecture continues. The students are more animated today, and she continues taking notes, scanning different tiles on the screen.

2:08 p.m. She is again watching the tile with the student and the child. The student lies on the couch and has the child in her camera screen. The child hugs the student and then climbs on top of the student and sits on her.

The lecture continues. The child continues to make occasional appearances, capturing both the student's and the observer's attention.

As the class ends, the instructor acknowledges the child's presence; "Who's our guest?" The student responds, "It's my little cousin." The instructor says hello to the child.

After Class

After students log off the Zoom session, the instructor, the peer mentor, and the graduate assistant discuss the students' experiences with college courses. The instructor and the peer mentor state that students, particularly in this course section, are struggling with the transition to college and the difference in expectations between high school and college regarding coursework. The instructor shares that one student had been emailing him about another instructor, stating the other instructor had been rude, but that wasn't the impression he had. He felt that the email was firm but fair.

The peer mentor indicates that her own transition to college had been difficult, as she had to learn how to do more work independently outside of class time and had to ask for help. The instructor and the peer mentor talk about the rigor of the coursework for students hoping to get into this program and the high number of students who won't pass some of the rigorous courses. The humanities course is one that the students mention as being particularly challenging. Another difficult course that students are currently taking is a science course that they need for their degree program.

The graduate assistant and the instructor also discuss the dynamic in the breakout room that was observed. The graduate assistant shares that the students didn't facilitate the discussion as instructed and were quiet for much of the time. The graduate assistant feels that the students appeared to look to her for direction. The instructor indicates that break-out rooms don't appear to be working with this group of students and that they need more direct facilitation and guidance. For the most part, these are lower-performing students. He believes that they aren't always highly self-motivated.

Unknown Audibles

The students are placed in a breakout room to work in small groups on an activity:

1:42 p.m. She enters the breakout room. The students are muted, not speaking with each other.

The students had been assigned a scenario and asked to use the university's website to find support resources. She scans the tiles. There are fewer to look through in the breakout rooms.

1:45 p.m. One student smiles, muted.

1:46 p.m. Another student unmutes and asks, "So what did you guys find?" A third student unmutes to respond: "I just went to the [campus resource] website." This student shares about some of the events that were on the calendar.

1:47 p.m. The peer mentor enters the room and asks students how they are doing. A student responds that the students are looking at the [campus resource] website. There is background music and one of the students says, "Why can't I find this shit?" The student quickly realizes that her microphone isn't muted and offers an *"oh, sorry"* as they mute their microphone.

Student Learning

Vocal class today. The instructor primes students to participate by asking them "If you could only eat one food for the rest of your life, what would it be?" Several students unmute or type in the chat box. The instructor concludes, "I feel like we are a starchy bunch."

Today's topic is Bloom's Taxonomy and learning styles. The instructor asks students about their study techniques. One student responds, "I take notes about what the instructor is saying, not just what is on the slides. Handwritten notes." Another student shares, "I read and highlight before the lecture and then print the PowerPoints and take some notes in class, but mostly I just listen. I am not awake at 8 a.m. in the morning."

The instructor talks about the different expectations faculty have in high school as compared to college.

A student unmutes, saying, "I like to take color-coded notes, but I also will ask myself questions out loud." Another student adds, "I like to create my own study sheets."

The instructor talks about her own experience while in college with studying and shares specific study techniques. One student seems disconnected from class, looking at something off screen. Another student unmutes herself and talks about her experience in a science class. "The professor has a lot of slides. I read them before class and then highlight things as I listen to the lecture." The instructor asks if anyone is struggling with any of their classes. After a long silence, one student unmutes and admits "I am struggling with the science class and the lab. They don't really connect. The class doesn't line up with the lab." A second student unmutes and encourages the first to "go to office hours with [the instructor]. It really helps and [the instructor] is really great." Two other students agree, and one of them mentions that the TA is hard to understand.

Because of the way this learning community is structured, most students in this class are in the same science lab. The instructor offers to create a discussion board in Blackboard or to create a Microsoft Teams chat for students to work together and ask each other questions. She also encourages students to create study groups and to reach out to the instructor. She emphasizes "professors do care and do want you to succeed."

The conversation shifts to an English class. A student volunteers that "there's a lot of essays and I am not really good at writing, so I start early and then go to the Writing Center and have a peer review it." The instructor thanks the student for sharing. The conversation continues. "Does anyone feel like the [social science class] should be common sense, but it isn't." A second student shares that the study guide was just given to the students today for a quiz that was released this afternoon. A third student steers back toward the science class. "I wish that [science] was the synchronous class and [social science] was the asynchronous class."

With fifteen minutes left in class time, the instructor asks students what would be more helpful to them during the remainder of class: breakout rooms to talk with each other about specific courses or to get updates from their peer mentor. There is no response from the students. "Ok, I will just let your peer mentor give you all some updates."

Class concludes with the instructor asking students if they would like a discussion board created in Blackboard where they can discuss courses and help each other. Several students nod yes.

Breakout Room

The lesson for the class centers on study habits. As the instructor asks students to share some of the techniques they use when studying, one of the students indicates that the humanities course the student is taking is particularly challenging. The student says, "It's not going to work out too well for me. I can't just sit in a Zoom room and just listen to the professor talk. [The instructor] just talks and has no words on the PowerPoints." Another student agrees. As the conversation continues, the instructor asks students to type in the chat box which course they feel they are having the most trouble with. As the students type in their answers, the majority of them indicate they are struggling with the humanities and science courses the most. The instructor then tells the students they will be divided into groups by course, and each group will go to a breakout room. The expectations for the time in the breakout rooms are for the students to talk about what's working and what's not working. The instructor indicates that the students should support each other by sharing which techniques they can use from their lesson to be more successful in the course. After the students are given instructions for the activity, the breakout rooms are opened and the students join.

She observes a breakout room with six students present. After all students have joined the room, one student unmutes and says, "Hello, everyone." Two of the other students also say hello and then there is silence. All the students are muted, and those students with their cameras on don't appear to be looking at the other group members. After a couple minutes of silence, one of the students asks what they are supposed to be doing. The students are told the instructions again, and one of the students indicates that the material is difficult to understand. Another student unmutes and says, "I am so unmotivated. I wait until the day of the class to skim through the lecture to find the answers to complete assignments." That's the extent of the interactions as the students sit in silence for the remaining time in the breakout rooms. She is surprised by the lack of interaction among students. The students have been given an opportunity to share their frustrations and experiences, yet they remain quiet. Some students have their cameras on, some don't, but all are muted and appear to be marking time until the end of the class. She wonders how her presence in the breakout rooms influences the students' experience. She's been observing for several weeks now. Do students see her as an "authority figure" in the room and therefore more hesitant to talk openly? Or are they simply using the breakout rooms as a way to zone out? How does the current virtual environment of the class impact students' connections to each other? She knows that the students in this one-credit class aren't all on campus or in the same dorm, which may make it more difficult for them to make connections in this virtual environment.

Disappearing Act

Toward the end of the semester, the peer mentor mentions to her that it had been hard for the students to remain engaged in their classes and the extracurricular learning experiences that were offered to the students. Even though there was an opportunity to win prizes for their attendance, there were only ten or fifteen submissions of proof of attendance. The peer mentors would remind them to attend events and to send feedback to the peer mentors or instructors, but the peer mentors felt that the students didn't want to attend. This peer mentor believes that the students didn't find these opportunities appealing. One of the other course sections was much more engaged, attending more out-of-class events and demonstrating more activity in their discussion group by submitting feedback and asking questions. It had been hard for the peer mentors to communicate with some of the students. The instructors would encourage the peer mentors to check up on students who were regularly absent from class, but frequently the students wouldn't reply to the messages. The peer mentor shares, "I guess being online people are able to just like not talk to you and then you're like, OK, well, I don't know where this person went."

High Hopes

Some stakeholders hoped for the emergency synchronous online courses to mimic the interpersonal dynamic of the face-to-face classroom, allowing students and instructors to interact and learn together. These expectations were met with disappointment early in the semester. The instructor tells her about the similarities and differences in student behaviors in previous years compared to the current year. The instructor indicates that current declines in attendance and participation are consistent with previous years. However, she also finds that there are different challenges in the Zoom environment than in a classroom environment. The instructor shares that she messages students privately in chat box about inappropriate behavior as she prefers not to call out students in class. However, the instructor has noted that there are behavioral challenges that are a concern. For example, the instructor privately messaged a couple of students in today's class, as she felt that students were not attentive to the guest speakers. One student indicated that the student's mic wasn't working properly after the instructor called on the student. The instructor tells her that she felt that the information wasn't accurate because the student still should have heard the question, and yet the student didn't respond until the student's roommate, who is also in this class, got up and spoke to the student.

Emergency Remote Instruction

Five minutes prior to the scheduled class start time she logs into the Zoom room. The virtual waiting room is enabled. Unlike in-person classes where students might be lingering in pairs or groups outside a locked classroom, waiting in Zoom world is a solo affair. It is silent; it is still.

At 8 a.m. on the dot, the virtual classroom opens with ninety-three participants. She notices many of the students' cameras turned on, albeit with no faces in them. Two minutes later, the instructor shares his screen. The slide reads "what is [field of study]." There is still no sound. The instructor begins lecturing, his sound going in and out. He announces that he only looks at the chat comments after class.

Meanwhile, in the chat, more than a dozen students report that the sound is going in and out for them. Finally, one student unmutes their microphone and alerts the instructor to the problem verbally, who reads the text on the current slide to test it. He then switches microphones and goes on with class. "I highly recommend spending more time reading and taking notes and less time texting each other during the meeting." The sound is still going in and out. She presumes this is because there are eighty-nine participants with cameras on.

A little while later, the instructor poses a question to the class. "How might you explain someone committing suicide?" A handful of students unmute themselves and reply with one-word answers. *How did one of our theorists explain suicide?* A few beats of silence, followed by the instructor's comment. "If you read the chapter, you would know this." Two students quickly unmute themselves and answer with responses from the text. The instructor repeats their responses to the class.

One student is up and doing something in the back of her room, maybe making coffee. Another student's camera shows a string of Christmas lights hanging from the ceiling of the room. Her face is obscured by her name on her video tile.

Students making coffee, Christmas lights on display, and faces obscured by digital displays of students' names: she notes these things as occurrences unique to virtual learning.

One student appears to be in a bed. Her video moves slightly, indicating that she may have the meeting pulled up on her phone. Yet another student is sharing a screen with another student. Are they in the library? Another student appears to be on her bed. Her body is horizontal. Light flashes on her face as if she's watching TV or a video on her phone. She rubs her face with her hand, and she pulls her comforter over her shoulder. Her head is propped on her hand, and it appears she is having a hard time keeping her eyes open.

Students lying in bed, consuming class through a phone, and watching TV: More idiosyncrasies of online synchronous learning. Are all of these students in the same class? Are they in the same learning community? They connect in the chat for seconds at a time, but otherwise there is no real in-class interaction between them, at least within Zoom, and specifically within its functions that are visible to all participants.

A half hour into class, a student in the chat asks if the sound is still going in and out. Several affirmative responses.

One student's camera is pointed toward the ceiling. The student angles it so that it points at her pillow and the upper right-hand quadrant of her face. It turns back up to her wall. Is she listening? Her camera keeps moving, finally stopping while pointed at the blinds in her residence hall room window. Her face is nowhere to be seen.

There are a few students who appear to be engaged. One is sitting up with her back straight, looking at her screen. She appears to be taking notes. The same is true for the student in the tile to the left of her: she seems alert and sitting up. Both faces are well lit. Cameras are steady, probably on laptops placed on a table or desk.

With ten minutes left in class, the instructor stops screen share, and she can hear him clicking through video tiles, calling out the names of folks who have their cameras turned off. At the same time, he encourages questions from the class. Students unmute themselves and ask about deadlines for quizzes, the reading assignment for next class, how deeply they should study the theories. One student takes visible notes as the instructor responds to her questions. She unmutes herself again, says "okay, thank you" and remutes herself.

Impressions

Some students continue to lie in bed during class with some falling asleep during the presentation of course information. After one class once all students had departed, the instructor talks with her about the reminder that was given to students about lying in the bed and asks her if she noticed how many of the students appeared to be inattentive during the class session. The instructor also asks her if she saw *that one student who was lying in bed also had a boy in same bed*. It's apparent that the instructor is shocked and dismayed. The instructor expresses concern about the impression that students lying in bed will have on faculty guest speakers who come to class to present.

Movement, Integration

Impact logic structures valid higher education research.[2] Impact makes possible the common sense of equations relating student engagement to retention and graduation rates and student retention from year to year and degree completion as measurable with student success. Within impact, student success can be tracked on a dashboard of measurable indicators: "Data informed decisions for student success—now that's a good idea!"[3] If impact is a measurable gain in student outcomes, dashboards can achieve nothing greater than their rendering. If progress is instead Coach Bennett's formulation of gradual, often imperceptible betterment,[4] there could be no such thing as a dashboard re/presenting student information system data on a given student. If progress names the value of Manning's focus on process, it names not a dashboard, or "the share of experience that is affirmed . . . because of what it is," but rather progress as "affirmed . . . because of how it affects experience in the making."[5] Visual representations of a static impact, even a static impact updated in as close to real time as possible, can never capture Coach Bennett's flavor of progress or Manning's flavor of process. Dashboards of impact are to a college education what a smartwatch is to an outdoor run: in attuning to the metrics, you miss not just the world around you but the myriad forms that progress takes otherwise.

When revaluing the ordinary, anecdotes must not become their own outcome. We can't live in impasses forever; this is the experience of late capitalism, wherein our attachments to desires that imperil us keep us endlessly chasing them, as the loss of the chase of these desires is as potentially harmful as the desire itself.[6] In the context of university classroom life, we paradoxically live in an impasse of impact. College actors chase impact because our desires have been routed as such; responsible actors desire data-driven college environments.[7] And yet, college actors never land on the properly *impacted* space. There is always a bigger impact to be had—a better impact, a broader impact. Impact promises certainty but delivers endless uncertainty. The ordinary must not become this type of outcome; we must not chase its impact in ways that lock us into cycles wherein we again desire university environments that foreclose possibilities of liberal education. Anecdotes are only valuable in so far as they remain rooted in unrouted movement. To be ordinary is to escape notice in most cases, to not be extraordinary, to largely escape comment, to be taken as everyday. But to reify the ordinary into its own outcome is to render it as abstracted and widgetized as impact. To progress is to move. The movement of the ordinary as progress is to move without a routing, without an end, and without the ordinary becoming an impediment itself to progress.

Integration comes into play here. Integration has many lives in educational literature: as a psychological concept referencing the interaction between individualized persons and otherwise separate environments,[8] as a term used in the early days of college impact studies that's roughly synonymous with engagement[9] and also as a key element of what learning communities and other high-impact practices are to produce: integrative learning.[10] Movement, integration, value. Integration is a movement of students and knowledge and competence across disciplinary boundaries and other structuring devices. Integration suffers the same fate when abstracted: the ordinary moves out of focus, becoming a by-product of the metric.

Integration comes not only to stand in for engagement but also for liberal education. All suffer similarly when understood through metrics rather than (or in place of) anecdotes. Liberal education becomes outcomes.[11] Engagement becomes the structuring device for one of the most well-known national surveys of students.[12] Integration becomes the presence of a shared assignment between two classes rather than the spark, the movement, the incitement of affect in everyday classroom life.

GroupMe Learning

While waiting for the class start time, the peer mentor shares with her that a student had attended one of her office hours. During the session, the student indicated that some of the students in the science class were messaging each other during the exams to share answers. The messaging group was set up by the peer mentor specifically for this learning community.

For What It's Worth

Today's guest speaker shares about the value of volunteering and service learning. There are twenty-two students logged onto the Zoom class; all of them have their cameras turned on. Two of them are only partially on camera with the tops of their heads. Three students have drinks, and two sit in darkened rooms. Another two are looking down, perhaps working on other coursework.

The guest speaker invites students to raise their physical hands-on camera if they have volunteered before. Almost all students raise their hands. The guest speaker encourages students to share in the chat box some volunteer work they have done. Answers include tutoring, food bank, Operation Smile, mission trip, working in a hospital, SPCA, and childcare at church.

"Why is it valuable to do service learning? Why is volunteering important?" Again, students type their answers in the chat. Gain experience. Build résumé. You can learn a lot from hands-on experience. To genuinely learn about the resources we have to help us when we are in need. The guest speaker invites specific students to unmute themselves to orally elaborate on their written answers. Students talk about how valuable these learning experiences can be, the value of knowing what resources are available, and the value of building social skills. The guest speaker, too, talks about the value of volunteering.

Three students are looking down at something. They appear to be writing. She is unsure if they are taking notes or perhaps working on other coursework or assignments. What value do students feel that this class holds? This learning community? What were they hoping to gain from it when it started? What about now?

Students are physically present—they are logged into Zoom at least—but are they cognitively present? Are they Engaged?

The guest speaker goes on to talk about ways that knowing about resources and volunteer experiences can be valuable to the students' future career goals. One of the students is still looking down, pencil or pen in hand. Another student is sitting by a window, looking outside. Yet another student is eating and looking away from their screen. It's unclear what the student is looking at. Perhaps they have logged into Zoom on their phone and are working on other assignments on their computer.

The guest speaker places her email address in the chat box. She asks students if they have any questions. There is no response, verbal or written.

Steering the Ship

Maybe learning communities operate within a kitchen filled with leaders. It's a chef's kitchen with shiny counters and top-of-the-line appliances. In this kitchen, faculty lead their courses. Departmental advisors sometimes lead recruiting efforts. The central learning community coordinating office administrators lead something else. The workshop facilitators lead the training of faculty. The graduate assistant leads the peer mentors (some of them, anyway).

There's emotional labor in the kitchen that is invisible in the finished meal. There's social risk related to the political landscape and implied hierarchies. There is pride and tensions and angst that lead to toes getting stepped on and feelings that get hurt.

Too many head chefs in the kitchen?

Some might say yes.

Mobile Learning

The convenience of synchronous, virtual classes means students can attend from anywhere they have internet access. Students attend this class sitting at their desks in their dorm rooms, from the local coffee shop with free Wi-Fi access, or at the beach while on vacation with their family.

Today, one student is attending class from inside a motor vehicle while sitting in the driver's seat. She hopes that the student is in a parked vehicle, but as she continues to observe, the camera angle falls to the side and reveals that the student is driving. She decides to spend more time observing this student.

1:55 p.m. The student in the vehicle repositions the camera. She turns it right side up and then turns it off altogether.

1:57 p.m. The student in the vehicle turns her camera back on and has repositioned the camera while it was off. It now appears as though the student's camera is in her lap with the camera positioned so that viewers are looking up at the student's face. Trees and shadows pass by the vehicle window.

1:59 p.m. The student is no longer in the Zoom session.

She wonders if the instructor placed the student back in the waiting room or removed her from the Zoom session.

The student doesn't return to the class session prior to the end of class, and this is probably best for safety reasons. But she wonders, isn't it better to miss the class than to try to attend while operating a vehicle? Why was this student attempting to multitask in this way?

Transitions

For many first-year students, the transition from high school to college is challenging regardless of the mode of course delivery. Used to the structure and expectations of high school classes, the transition to college is difficult as instructors expect them to be more independent. Early in the semester the students express concerns about their transition to college and the instructor gives them time in a breakout room in small groups to talk about their struggles.

Student 1: "My high school was small."

Student 2: "I agree." There is a brief discussion about the small size of their graduating classes.

Student 3: "The workload is different."

Student 4: "Being away from my family"

Student 1: "My biggest challenge is not getting behind—I wasn't a studier in high school"

Student 2: "Asking for help [. . .] I always want to do things on my own."

Student 3: "Self-motivation is my biggest challenge"

Student 5: "My biggest challenge is procrastination."

Student 3: "I feel you with that."

Welcome

As formal educational environments in the United States transition to emergency remote instruction as a response to the COVID-19 pandemic, students and instructors experience ambiguity and uncertainty. Faculty are encouraged to ensure that this transition is as smooth as possible. They should create a sense of normalcy—a new normal—and class environments should be as similar to face-to-face classrooms as possible. As the semester begins, the instructors attempt to provide an atmosphere of normalcy in setting the tone for the semester, just as they would in the face-to-face environment.

It's the first Zoom session of the semester for this course. All students have their cameras on, and all are facing their screens. The instructor welcomes everyone and provides an outline for the class session. She then introduces the peer mentor. During this introduction, the instructor makes a joke about the fact that the peer mentor was in the class last year, saying, "[The peer mentor] can attest to what a mean instructor I am."

The instructor continues, "You are all part of a learning community." The instructor explains what a learning community is. She discusses the classes that students may be taking together and emphasizes that the benefits of the community are learning collaboratively with students with similar goals. The instructor ends the introduction with assurances to students that even though they are learning virtually this year, the faculty and staff are hoping to create the supportive and inviting feeling expected within a learning community. The instructor says, "You are in the right spot. You are welcome here."

Week 12

At 8 a.m. they are let into the Zoom room. Nearly twenty students are either absent or late. Two minutes later, the instructor locks the virtual classroom. In the virtual world, this means students are unable to knock on the classroom door to seek admittance. The instructor begins class by calling out students he can't see whether due to darkness or due to their camera not being turned on. He unsuccessfully calls on one student three times. When she fails to respond he removes her from the Zoom room.

The instructor opens the class for any questions students may have. One student unmutes herself to ask about the final exam.

Lecture goes on.

Midway through class, the instructor pauses his lecture to ask students about what theory is most relevant to the concept he was explaining. As he goes silent, a blaring TV can be heard through someone's microphone. The instructor calls out to students, saying, "You all should be muted. And you shouldn't have the TV blasting!"

Lecture continues.

A few minutes later, the instructor asks students if anyone ever googled their symptoms. One student raises her hand. The instructor calls on her, and she shares going to WebMD and looking up "shortness of breath," thinking she was experiencing a heart attack.

The instructor concludes lecture one minute past time. "What's due Thursday night?" One student responds with the correct answer. The instructor reiterates that this assignment is 10 percent of the grade. Two minutes past time, the instructor tells students he hopes they have a peaceful break. Students depart the Zoom room. Finally, there are only two students remaining, both asleep.

The instructor removes them from the Zoom room.

Re/Valuing the Ordinary

If you agree that re/valuing learning communities (and student engagement, and higher education) is worth entertaining, might we suggest one mode of entertaining this is to re/value the ordinary practices of our colleges and universities.

The ordinary here takes on a meaning grounded in affect theory and cultural studies, but it's really nothing more than what it sounds like. If the exceptional grabs our attention because of its deviation from expected norms, the ordinary conforms to our expectations. It does not grab our attention. These anecdotes express the white noise of everyday life, the practices we take for granted, the unremarkable. Research that metricizes the value of college and university environments extracts otherwise ordinary moments of college life and converts them into discrete and recombinable units to create them as extra-ordinary. Even research on learning communities that is qualitative in nature typically redounds to schemes of coding meaningful bits of information, collecting codes, creating themes, and presenting the details of the ordinary via this extraction.[13] The ordinary here does not stand alone. It's impossible to escape the fact that these are the anecdotes that began as our observations that we then selected for their glow and finally rendered in literary form. The ordinary here does stand as singular. The singular is that which escapes categorization.[14] The singular is not unique. This is evident throughout these anecdotes, as there are parts that no doubt have resonated with the personal experience of readers with experience in college environments, or in teaching and learning environments generally, formal or informal. There are pieces of these moments that are also pieces of your moments. The anecdotes here are singular combinations of what our social world can make at any moment, with the imperceptible possibilities of alternate realities included. These anecdotes did not exist in the past and will not exist again. They exist here in these pages as artifacts. We present to you a graveyard of artifacts. To revalue them is not simply to reprint them here as anecdotes instead of data-driven truth. Rather, it is to develop practices of attunement such that our time and energy in every moment orients to anecdotes instead of immersing ourselves in cultures of evidence to properly datafy classroom (and college) life.[15] To the extent higher education can attune to the ordinary in every moment, a path exists to re/value practices like learning communities beyond their value through metrics.

Re/valuations of the ordinary are "attempts at touching what remains elusive. A quality in the between, an interval that cannot quite be articulated . . . the [quality] of an experience that cannot be reduced to the sum of its parts."[16] These moments seem inconsequential, but how could they be? Consequence—in one form, the outcomes that higher education values—cannot be anything outside of an accumulation of these anecdotes. We overlook the ordinary in search of meaningful information through mathematical aggregations of these anecdotes. The ordinary is not unique, and it is also not general. It is incapable of being quantitatively or qualitatively aggregated. The yet-to-come for research on college impact and higher education research broadly is this: to enact a values system of the ordinary that spins its webs in everyday educational lives.

Transitions, Too

Despite expectations set on day one of the course, the comfort and familiarity of the home environments often lulled students into a relaxed and casual demeanor that may have been construed as complacency by instructors more comfortable with face-to-face instruction. She observes a student lying on the bed under the blanket while other students aren't fully visible on screen with only tops of heads or half of their faces visible. The instructor says, "I know it's 11:00 and some of you are tired, but I need you to sit up. I need to see your face."

Interlude: June Angst

They are 55 minutes into a 90-minute workshop geared toward (re)calibrating the faculty who will teach learning communities in fall 2020. This workshop, like many meetings around the world on this day, is held via videoconferencing technology. This workshop occurs during the intermission between the 2019–20 academic year (a time characterized by in-person interactions in State U. learning communities) and the 2020–21 academic year (a time that would be dominated by online interactions at State U. and elsewhere). Neither the faculty nor the five facilitators are cognizant of what may come. This is a space filled with uncertainty and unease.

They are now thirteen minutes behind schedule. In the chat box, one of the facilitators writes: "This summer, the learning community team will be continually available to help with designing online aspects for the learning community and offering follow up optional workshops on ways of translating these into online experiences/practices."

None of the instructors acknowledge this comment. Microphones remain muted. The chat box stays empty.

Nevertheless, there's a distinct buzzing in the Zoom room. A quiet murmur, barely discernible, yet obnoxious in its inability to be captured and calmed. A vibe of concentration, concern, and consternation. A feeling of uncertainty and questioning permeates the screaming silences, begging the facilitators to acknowledge the proverbial elephant.

" 'I don't know' seems an acceptable answer."

As the workshop concludes, the session host thanks facilitators and reminds faculty attendees they must attend both workshops to get the first half of their stipend for teaching a learning community.

Ordinary Impacts

How can we come to value progress, the movement of the impasse, over impact? Re/valuing anecdotes is one option, so long as they retain their attachment to the real and resist becoming structuring devices of their own. To develop questions of value unanswerable by impact measurements,[17] we attune to insignificant practices around us. We look first to experiences that glow, moments that we don't quite know what to make of, moments that stand out for reasons other than their coherence into a VALUE rubric or component of a high-impact practice.[18] In higher education, this attunement incites liberal education through valuing ordinary practices that escape the capture of measurement.

The ordinary is within taken-for-granted structuring devices like high-impact practices. This is imperceptible impact. This is progress as impasse. When the value of higher education is known and lived through structuring devices like high-impact practices, student engagement, and integrative learning, they route our values and overdetermine our practices. Impasses open us to the possibilities that exist for progress within and in excess of metrics. Impasses live in each anecdote.

Impasses themselves do not contain the map to our liberation. There is no outside of our world of impact, only messy paths through. Impasses are nightmares, impasses are hope, impasses contain every existing moment worth valuing and every existing harm. Impasses contain the value of living at the surface, reducing and eliminating abstractions like structuring devices and data. We must revalue making judgments and decisions in higher education not from abstractions, not data-driven or data-informed, but creations with, from, and through messy entanglements with the world. There is no structuring device worth settling into, returning to, or reclaiming. Impact is not made better through transforming it into full-cycle assessment, the student success movement, predictive analytics, or the next structuring device to come. Anecdotes open anecdotes. We experiment with our worlds and do better tomorrow. An affirmative politics means nothing more than this.[19] We value impasse over impact. We live with the radical collective and individual responsibility that this valuing confers. And tomorrow, we create the world anew.

Afterword

Values

A revaluing of higher education broadly—and campus classroom life specifically—is a move to radically resist the abstraction of practice. Structuring devices like high-impact practices (even data itself) are the making-perceptible of progress. Just as impact happens, perceptibility happens. Of course this is exactly what we did here to some degree. As much as we resisted using structuring devices to do so, still we made the progress of learning communities at State U. perceptible. We made these ordinary moments perceptible through anecdote and then moved on to the next. We sought that *what next* of progress. Where a structuring device like impact would route the path of this perceptibility according to its own image, *what next* is an orientation to difference: good, bad, or otherwise. *What next* within an affirmative politics is an orientation to imperceptible progress.

To this end, this book makes a case for infinite new normals. Stability is not a bad thing, but the routing of daily practice that structuring devices enact limits, by design, all of our futures. Normality is one more structuring device for our world, one whose existence in various forms long predates the pandemic. The normal is a concept that has generated decades of critique from queer studies and elsewhere.[1] Persistent calls for a new normal express a desire for stability in an unprecedented world.[2] Our world was never so stable to begin with, and there are many aspects of pandemic life that remain much too within precedent. Persistent calls for a new normal also ignore the fact that classroom life in many ways was strangely stable. Despite the upheaval of campus life and the material differences between in-person and synchronous online classes, at State U., the boredom generated by the lecture format was quite stable. Heads on desks before the pandemic became students in bed during. Locked lecture halls became closed Zoom rooms. Textbook publishing company–generated slide shows persisted. We do not seek a new and improved normal. We seek the *what next*.

Against the abstractions of impact, impasses privilege fleshy values and imperceptible progress. Impasses are lived spaces of movement (engagement, integration, impact) that resist forces that might categorize, name, and stabilize them (Engagement, Integration, Impact). Ultimately, stability comes.[3] We desire it. To value the impasses of higher education is to continually seek the next anecdote and open the next question. Doing so does not eliminate abstractions of practice but rather reorients our energies elsewhere.[4] As we have demonstrated here, this reorientation to the impasse is intensely practical. We practice impasses every day. This revaluation of higher education exists here and now. Attune. Create.

Notes

Introduction

1. Throughout this book, when we refer to high-impact practices, we are referring specifically to the set of practices enumerated by Kuh, *High-Impact Practices*.

2. Kuh, *High-Impact Practices*.

3. See, for example, Commission on the Future of Higher Education, *A Test of Leadership*; Denna, "Business Model"; Ewell, "Capture the Ineffable"; Postsecondary Value Commission, *Equitable Value*; Study Group on the Conditions of Excellence in American Higher Education, *Involvement in Learning*.

4. Ahmed, *Queer Phenomenology*. See Smithers, "Reconceptualizing Impact" for a reading of Ahmed's *orientations* through poststructural theory.

5. American Association of University Professors, *COVID-19 and Governance*; Kezar, DePaola, and Scott, *Gig Academy*.

6. Bauman, "Year of Losses"; Bauman, "Just Rewards"; Bauman, "Pandemic Pushed Workers Out"; Burke, "Campus Zero"; Carlson et al., "Forced Out"; Friga, "University Budgets"; Gardner, "Great Contraction"; Hubler, "Colleges Slash Budgets"; Kelchen, "Permanent Budget Cuts"; Pettit, "Contingent Faculty"; Whitford, "Wave of Furloughs."

7. Mintz, "Not Return Old Normal"; Schapiro, "Not Return to Normal."

8. See Newfield, *Great Mistake*; Potter, "Save Higher Education."

9. Braidotti, *Nomadic Theory*, Manning, *Minor Gesture*.

10. For the development of college impact as a tool for studying college environments, see Astin, "College Impact Part One" and "College Impact Part Two." The production of impact as the common sense of higher education research emerges with Feldman and Newcomb, *Impact of College*, as well as the work of Astin, *Four Critical Years* and Tinto, "Dropout," and crystallizes with the various volumes of *How College Affects Students* (Pascarella and Terenzini, *How College Affects Students*; Pascarella and Terenzini, *How College Affects Students Vol. 2*; Mayhew et al., *How College Affects Students Vol. 3*).

11. See, for example, College of Human Sciences & Education, *IMPACT*; Darden College of Education and Professional Studies, *Making an Impact*; Doherty, "100 Years."

12. See, for example, Barger, "College Orientation"; College of St. Scholastica, "Making an Impact."

13. Esters, "Making an Impact"; University of Colorado, *Making an Impact*.

14. See, for example, Boggs, "Making an Impact"; Payne, "Making an Impact"; Virginia Peninsula Community College, "Making an Impact."

15. Astin, "College Impact Part One."

16. This is the definition of a high-impact practice, a practice that, through its ability to increase student engagement, increases retention and graduation. See Kuh, *High-Impact Practices*.

17. Regele, "Pedagogy and Profit?"

18. Kuh, *High-Impact Practices*.

19. Amoore, *Politics of Possibility*; Massumi, *Ontopower*; Watermark Insights, "Artificial and Human Intelligence."

20. For an exemplar of the completion agenda, see Complete College America, *No Room for Doubt*.

21. Watermark Insights, "Success Coaching."

22. Babb, "Onboarding and Enrollment Redesign."

23. Berlant, *Cruel Optimism*.

24. We follow Smith et al.'s definition of learning communities here: "a variety of curricular approaches that intentionally link or cluster two or more courses, often around an interdisciplinary theme or problem, and enroll a common cohort of students. They represent an intentional restructuring of students' time, credit, and learning experiences to build community, enhance learning, and foster connections among students, faculty, and disciplines. At their best, learning communities practice pedagogies of active engagement and reflection." Smith et al., *Learning Communities*, 20.

25. Hill, "Learning Communities"; Kuh, *High-Impact Practices*; Meiklejohn, "Wisconsin's Experimental Colleges"; Paige et al., *Learning Community Experience*; Zhao and Kuh, "Adding Value." See Chapter 2 of Smith et al. *Learning Communities* for an excellent synthesis of the history of learning communities in the 20th century.

26. cf. National Survey of Student Engagement, *Experiences That Matter*; National Survey of Student Engagement, *Engagement Insights*.

27. Stewart, *Ordinary Affects*, 3.

28. See, for example, National Survey of Student Engagement, *Engagement Insights*.

29. Coburn, "Rethinking Scale"; Macgilchrist, Potter, and Williamson, "Shifting Scales."

30. Kuh and O'Donnell, "Ensuring Quality."

31. Sharpe, *In the Wake*; *Ordinary Notes*.

32. Berlant, *Cruel Optimism*.

33. Berlant, *Cruel Optimism*, 199.

34. Berlant, *Cruel Optimism*, 4.

35. Hatch, "Black Box"; Hatch and Bohlig, "Empirical Typology"; Holt and Nielson, "Learning Communities"; Love, "Current State."

36. Hill, "Learning Communities"; Meiklejohn, "Wisconsin's Experimental Colleges"; Smith, "Growing National Movement."

37. Berlant and Stewart, *The Hundreds*; Stewart, *Ordinary Affects*.

38. On the allure of causality, see Barad, *Meeting the Universe Halfway*; Kuntz, *The Responsible Methodologist*.

39. Fineman, "History of the Anecdote," 56.

40. Gagliardi, Parnell, and Carpenter-Hubin, *Analytics Revolution*. See also Berlant, *Cruel Optimism* on crisis ordinariness.

41. While you will be moved, affect is irreducibly social as well as irreducibly qualitative. See Massumi, *99 Theses*. Your experience of movement is the experience of plugging into a social force.

42. Freeman, *Modes of Thinking* on diagrammatical thinking; Gullion, *Diffractive Ethnography*; Jackson and Mazzei, *Thinking With Theory*; Stewart, *Ordinary Affects*. Yes, this book is written in a tradition that questions the very utility of methodology, including ethnography. However, we believe that some legibility in naming our practices is both accurate and hopefully helpful to those less familiar with poststructural theory and postqualitative inquiry. In this way, we align with Wolgemuth et al., "Radical Uncertainty is Not Enough."

43. Kuh et al., *What Matters*.

44. Hill, "Learning Communities"; Kuh, *High-Impact*.

45. Stewart, *Ordinary Affects*, 5. Fineman describes this quality as well. For him, the anecdote "possesses [a] peculiar and eventful force." Fineman, "History of the Anecdote," 57.

46. Gregg and Siegworth, *Affect Theory Reader*; Massumi, *99 Theses*; Stewart, *Ordinary Affects*.

47. Stewart, *Ordinary Affects*, 6.

48. Berlant, *Cruel Optimism*; Braidotti, *Nomadic Theory*; Manning, *Minor Gesture*.

49. "A rhizome has no beginning or end; it is always in the middle, between things, interbeing, *intermezzo* . . . the fabric of the rhizome is the conjunction, 'and . . . and . . . and . . .' This conjunction carries enough force to shake and uproot the verb 'to be.' Where are you going? Where are you coming from? What are you heading for? These are totally useless questions. Making a clean slate, starting or beginning again from ground zero, seeking a beginning or foundation—all imply a false conception of voyage and movement (a conception that is methodical, pedagogical, initiatory, symbolic . . .) . . . . establish a logic of

the AND, overthrow ontology, do away with foundations, nullify endings and beginnings . . . the middle is by no means an average; on the contrary, it is where things pick up speed." Deleuze and Guattari, *A Thousand Plateaus*, 25.

50. Braidotti, *Nomadic Subjects*.

51. Stewart, *Ordinary Affects*, 5.

52. Stewart, *Ordinary Affects*.

53. Berlant, *Cruel Optimism*; Mol, *Body Multiple*.

54. Kuh and O'Donnell, *Ensuring Quality*.

55. See Fineman, "History of the Anecdote," 56–57.

56. Brown, *Undoing the Demos*, Massumi, *Ontopower*.

57. Massumi, *99 Theses*.

Chapter One

1. "In order to be recognizable, you have to answer the call to order—and that the only genuine and authentic mode of living in the world is to be recognizable within the terms of order. But, it's kind of like that thing where you walk into class, you're the teacher and you get there a couple minutes early and there are people milling around and there's a conversation already going on, and some of them might be talking about stuff you might be talking about in class and some of them might be talking about something completely different—and at the same time, I've been thinking about something, either what we've been talking about in class or something completely different. My position, at that moment, what I am supposed to do is at a certain point become an instrument of governance. What I'm supposed to do is to call that class to order, which presupposes that there is no actual, already existing organization happening, that there's no study happening before I got there, that there was no study happening, no planning happening. I'm calling it to order, and then something can happen—then knowledge can be produced. That's the presumption." See Harney and Moten, *The Undercommons*, 124–25.

2. Where we were able to capture direct quotations in our observation notes or from interviews or focus groups, we stylize them in "quotation marks." Where we paraphrased the words of our participants in our observation notes and reprint these paraphrasings verbatim here, we stylize them as *italicized*.

3. Ahmed, *Queer Phenomenology*; Smithers, "Reconceptualizing Impact."

4. Astin, "Student Involvement"; Bowden, Tickle, and Naumann, "Four Pillars"; Hatch, "Black Box"; Kahu, "Framing Student Engagement"; Kuh, "What Student Affairs"; Kuh, "What We're Learning"; Kuh et al., *What Matters*; Macfarlane and Tomlinson, "Critical and Alternative"; Wolf-Wendel, Ward, and Kinzie, "Tangled Web"; Zepke, "Student Engagement."

5. Soldner, Lee, and Duby, "Welcome."

6. Tinto, "Impact of Learning Communities."

7. National Survey of Student Engagement, *Engagement Insights.*

8. National Survey of Student Engagement, *Experiences That Matter.*

9. Tinto, "Learning Better Together."

10. Ribera, Miller, and Dumford, "Peer Belonging."

11. Engstrom and Tinto, "Learning Better Together."

12. Jaffee, "Peer Cohorts."

13. The title of this anecdote is a refrain of Deleuze and Guattari's body without organs. Deleuze and Guattari, *A Thousand Plateaus.*

14. Berlant, *Cruel Optimism.*

15. American Association of Colleges and Universities, *Integrative Learning.*

16. Keeling, *Queer Times.*

17. Kuh, *High-Impact Practices.*

18. Panos and Astin, "Attrition."

19. See, for example, Newman, *Idea of a University.*

20. On this last point, athletic progress, we can't recommend enough an outside-the-box source on this (outside-the-box in relation to sources cited in academic texts that is): Nike' s "Next Long Run" guided run, available through the Nike Run Club app. Over the forty-two minutes of this run, Coach Chris Bennett speaks very convincingly on just the point of this entire section—progress is many times imperceptible, and to hold yourself to a vision of progress defined only by measures like distance run or pace is to flatten experience. This section is as indebted to Coach Bennett's words in this run as they are to the other traditional academic sources.

21. With Coach Bennett's thoughts as a starting line, there is a long tradition of the importance of the imperceptible in poststructural thought and works taking up this thought in education research. See, for example, Braidotti, *Nomadic Subjects*; Braidotti, *The Posthuman*; de Freitas, "Calculating Matter;' de Freitas & Curinga, "New Materialist Approaches"; de Freitas & Ferrara, "Ontology of Learning"; Deleuze, *Difference and Repetition*; Deleuze, *Logic of Sense*; Deleuze and Guattari, *A Thousand Plateaus*; Foucault, *History of Sexuality Vol. 1*; Koopman, *Genealogy as Critique*; Manning, "Pragmatics of the Useless"; Springgay & Truman, *Walking Methodologies*; St. Pierre, "New Empiricisms"; St. Pierre, "Post Qualitative Inquiry."

22. Everyday practices are "scattered all along duration . . . Thus to eliminate the unforeseen or expel it from calculation as an illegitimate accident and an obstacle to rationality is to interdict the possibility of a living and 'mythical' practice of the city." De Certeau, *Everyday Life*, 203.

23. An imperceptibility from the point of view of data-driven culture that is; anecdotes hold a connection to the real that data cannot. Fineman, "History of the Anecdote."

24. Berlant, *Cruel Optimism.*

25. Kuh, *High-Impact Practices*; Massumi, *99 Theses*.

26. Jaffee, "Peer Cohorts."

27. The title of this anecdote is a refrain on Tatum, *Black Kids*.

Chapter Two

1. The title of this anecdote is from Deleuze and Guattari, *A Thousand Plateaus*, 21.

2. Kuh, "What Student Affairs"; Kuh et al., *What Matters*.

3. Kuh et al., *What Matters*.

4. American Association of Colleges and Universities, *Integrative Learning*, 1.

5. This is the seventh of eight key elements and examples of high-impact practices, "opportunities to discover relevance of learning through real-world applications." Kuh and O'Donnell, *Ensuring Quality*, 10.

6. Our use of entanglement here follows Karen Barad's usage: "The point is not merely that there is a web of causal relations that we are implicated in and that there are consequences to our actions. We are a much more intimate part of the universe than any such statement implies. If what is implied by 'consequences' is a chain of events that follow one upon the next, the effects of our actions rippling outward from their point of origin well after a given action is completed, then to say that there are consequences to our actions is to miss the full extent of the interconnectedness of being. Future moments don't follow present ones like beads on a string. Effect does not follow cause hand over fist, transferring the momentum of our actions from one individual to the next like balls on a billiards table. There is no discrete 'I' that precedes our actions. Our (intra)actions matter—each one reconfigures the world in its becoming—and yet they never leave us; they are sedimented into our becoming, they become us. And yet even in our becoming there is no 'I' separate from the intra-active becoming of the world. Causality if an entangled affair: it is a matter of cutting things together and apart (within and as part of phenomena)." Barad, *Meeting the Universe Halfway*, 394.

7. Engstrom and Tinto, "Learning Better Together"; Zhao and Kuh, "Adding Value."

8. Jaffee, "Peer Cohorts"; Stanwood and Dunlap, "Assessment Chase."

9. Engstrom and Tinto, "Learning Better Together."

10. Ribera, Miller, and Dumford, "Peer Belonging" or Arensdorf and Naylor-Tincknell, "Beyond Traditional Retention Data"?

11. Pike, Kuh, and McCormick, "Contingent Relationship" or Huba et al., "Assessment's Role?"

12. Tinto, "Impact of Learning Communities."

13. Astin, "Student Involvement."

14. Berlant, *Cruel Optimism*, 199.

15. The title of this anecdote is a refrain on Foucault, *Order of Things*.

Chapter Three

1. Adams, Murphy, and Clarke, "Anticipation"; Amsler and Facer, "Contesting Anticipatory Regimes"; Berlant, *Cruel Optimism*; Groves, "Emptying the Future."

2. McMahon, *Higher Learning*.

3. Deleuze, "Postscript," Raunig, *Dividuum*.

4. Jarke and Breiter, "Datafication of Education"; van Dijck, "Datafication, Dataism, and Dataveillance."

5. Deleuze, *Difference and Repetition*.

6. See also Manning, *Minor Gesture*.

7. Betty, "*L Word* Theme," 0:59.

8. This word is imperfect. The colloquial sense of affect is what works best here, but in this book, we define affect as social, not individual. The colloquial *vibes* would also work here.

9. Manning, "Radical Pedagogy," 48.

10. Manning, "Radical Pedagogy," 48.

11. For example, American Association of Colleges and Universities, *Valid Assessment*.

12. Smithers, "Define and Measure."

13. Manning, "Pragmatics of the Useless," 105.

14. Roth, "Pragmatic Liberal Education."

15. Gregg, *Counterproductive*

16. See Berlant, *Cruel Optimism*.

17. Farnham and Yarmolinsky, *Rethinking Liberal Education*.

18. Zakaria, *In Defense*.

19. Mulcahy, *Educated Person*.

20. Siegworth and Gregg, "Inventory of Shimmers," 2.

21. Manning, *Minor Gesture*; Smithers, "Preemption."

22. Manning, *Minor Gesture*, 227.

23. Betty, "*L Word* Theme," 1:00.

24. "*Affect resonates. Measure indexes.* These two modes are processually interlinked, across their difference." Massumi, *99 Theses*, 48.

25. See, for example, Newman, *Idea of a University*, 102–3.

26. Manning, "Pragmatics of the Useless."

27. In the *Real Housewives of Atlanta* Season 6 reunion special, cast member NeNe Leakes dropped this knowledge that continues to circle the internet: "I said what I said." (Cohen, "Reunion Special 3.")

28. Arcade Fire, "Wasted Hours," 0:00.

29. Arcade Fire, "Wasted Hours," 1:31.

Chapter Four

1. Kuh et al., *Student Success in College*, x.
2. Kuh et al., *Student Success in College*.
3. Kuh et al., *Student Success in College*, 9.
4. Kuh et al., *Student Success in College*, 9.
5. Astin, "Student Involvement"; Kuh et al., *Student Success in College*.
6. "Fitter, healthier, and more productive. / A pig, in a cage, on antibiotics" (Radiohead, "Fitter Happier," 1:43).
7. Kuh et al., *Student Success in College*.
8. "Statistical inquiry . . . 'finds' only the homogenous. The power of its calculations lies in its ability to divide, but it is precisely through this ana-lytic fragmentation that it loses sight of what it claims to seek and represent." de Certeau, *Ordinary Life*, xviii.
9. Stewart, *Ordinary Affects*, 19.
10. Berlant, "Intuitionists"; Massumi, *Parables*; Robinson and Kutner, "Affective Turn"; Spinoza, *Ethics*; Stewart, *Ordinary Affects*.
11. Massumi, *Parables*, 32–33.
12. Daza and Gershon, "Beyond Ocular Inquiry"; Gershon, "Vibrational Affect."
13. Braidotti, *Posthuman*.
14. Stewart, *Ordinary Affects*.
15. For agreement on this point from two different vantage points, see Perna, "Throwing Down the Gauntlet," and Snaza, "Ethologies of Education."
16. MacLure, "Researching Without Representation"; Wells et al., "How We Know."
17. Kuh, "What We're Learning"; Kuh et al., *Connecting the Dots*.
18. Astin, "Student Involvement"; Chickering and Gamson, "Seven Principles"; Kuh, "What Student Affairs."
19. Bowden, Tickle, and Naumann, "Four Pillars"; Kuh et al., *Student Success Puzzle*; Zilvinskis, Masseria, and Pike, "Student Engagement."
20. Kuh, "What We're Learning"; Wolf-Wendel, Ward, and Kinzie, "Tangled Web."
21. Macfarlane and Tomlinson, "Critical and Alternative."
22. Tukibayeva and Gonyea, "High-Impact Practices," 34.
23. See Smith, "Magnets and Seekers."
24. McConnell and Rhodes, *VALUE Report*, 17.
25. Musoba, Jones, and Nicholas, "Open Door," 730.
26. "This is why productivity has become such an accommodating capsule for contemporary notions of freedom: being productive, we embrace a pressing

sense of responsibility to carry out tasks that appear obvious and necessary in a broader catalogue of things that always need doing. The effect of this circularity is to obviate the need for frank conversations about morality or virtue, which can be related only to the distribution of work and wealth at a time of growing inequality." Gregg, *Counterproductive*, 19.

27. Kuh, *High-Impact Practices*.

28. Hoover, "Our Relationship."

29. McKay, *The Big Short*.

30. Simon, *The Wire*.

31. Jones, "How the Wire"; Saraiya, "15 Years Later"; Sheffield, "100 Greatest."

32. Cukier and Mayer-Schönberger, "Dictatorship of Data."

33. In such a redefinition of value, or revaluation, "the unquantifiable within experience can only be taken into account if we begin with a mode of inquiry that refutes initial categorization." Manning, *Minor Gesture*, 134. See also Manning's concept of the infrathin.

34. See Note 179, Sharpe, *Ordinary Notes*, 254.

35. MacLure, "Researching Without Representation."

36. No matter your current position or location, reader, public universities are indeed our universities, as are public community colleges and all other forms of public higher education.

37. Here we point you back to the preface, where this intention was set.

38. Lenning and Ebbers, "Powerful Potential."

39. Brian Massumi's Thesis 86 reverberates here. Massumi, *99 Theses*, 103.

40. A work of art; see Manning, *Minor Gesture*, 28.

41. Manning, *Minor Gesture*, 203.

42. All bodies inquire. This wording is to distinguish acts of inquiry from subject positions and professional titles of researcher.

43. See also Braidotti, *Nomadic Theory*, on affirmative ethics, especially Part 4.

44. Research creation "creates new values, values that exceed use-value, values that have not yet invented their use. They don't yet know what they owe." See Manning, *Minor Gesture*, 218. In this section Manning directly draws on the work of Harney and Moten, *The Undercommons,* among others.

45. Fineman, "History of the Anecdote."

46. la paperson, *Third University;* Lorenz, "If You're So Smart"; Miller and Morphew, "Merchants of Optimism."

47. Harney and Moten, *Undercommons*; la paperson, *Third University*.

Chapter Five

1. Holy See, *Order for Funerals*, 46.

2. Mayhew, et al., *How College Affects Students*.

3. Morris, "Mining Data," 185, emphasis in original.

4. Nike, "Next Long Run."

5. Manning, "Pragmatics of the Useless," 103.

6. Berlant, *Cruel Optimism*.

7. Culp and Dungy, *Culture of Evidence*. See also Gregg, *Counterproductive*.

8. Individualized persons or laboratory rats, see Mowrer and Ullman, "Integrative Learning."

9. Tinto, "Dropout"; Wolf-Wendel, Ward, and Kenzie, "Tangled Web."

10. National Survey of Student Engagement, *Experiences That Matter*.

11. American Association of Colleges and Universities, *VALUE Rubrics*.

12. National Survey of Student Engagement, *Engagement Insights*.

13. Kuntz, *Responsible Methodologist*.

14. Deleuze, *Difference and Repetition*.

15. Ahmed, *Queer Phenomenology*; Gagliardi, Parnell, and Carpenter-Hubin, *Analytics Revolution*; Jarke and Breiter, "Datafication of Education"; Smithers, "Reconceptualizing Impact"; van Dijck, "Datafication, Dataism, and Dataveillance."

16. Manning, "Pragmatics of the Useless," 99.

17. This is also to say in excess of neoliberalism (Brown, *Undoing the Demos*) and control (Deleuze, "Postscript").

18. American Association of Colleges and Universities, *VALUE Rubrics*; Kuh and O'Donnell, *Ensuring Quality*.

19. Braidotti, *Nomadic Theory*.

Afterword

1. We will not attempt to cite entire disciplines here, but for those looking for a way into this conversation, see Ahmed, *Queer Phenomenology*.

2. See, for example, Burbules and Gunsalus, "Dealing with the Now"; Chronicle Staff, "Unprecedented Crisis"; Diep, "Covid 'New Normal;'" Hoover, "Extending Deposit Deadlines"; Lederman, "Shift to Remote Teaching"; Mintz, "Not Return Old Normal"; Schapiro, "Not Return to Normal."

3. "Arrive at the magic formula we all seek—PLURALISM = MONISM—via all the dualisms that are the enemy, an entirely necessary enemy, the furniture we are forever rearranging." Deleuze and Guattari, *A Thousand Plateaus*, 20–21.

4. Ahmed, *Queer Phenomenology*; Smithers, "Reconceptualizing Impact."

Bibliography

Adams, Vincanne, Michelle Murphy, and Adele E. Clarke. "Anticipation: Techno-science, Life, Affect, Temporality." *Subjectivity* 28 (2009): 246–65. https://doi.org/10.1057/sub.2009.18.

Ahmed, Sara. *Queer Phenomenology: Orientations, Objects, Others*. Durham, NC: Duke University Press, 2006.

American Association of Colleges and Universities. *Integrative Learning VALUE Rubric*. Accessed December 11, 2023. https://d38xzozy36dxrv.cloudfront.net/qa/content/user-photos/Offices/OCPI/VALUE/VALUERubric-Integrative-LearningPreviewOnly.pdf.

American Association of Colleges and Universities. *Valid Assessment of Learning in Undergraduate Education*. Accessed December 11, 2023. https://www.aacu.org/value.

American Association of Colleges and Universities. VALUE Rubrics. Accessed December 11, 2023. https://www.aacu.org/initiatives/value-initiative/value-rubrics.

American Association of University Professors. *Special Report: COVID-19 and Academic Governance*. Washington, DC: American Association of University Professors, May 2019. https://www.aaup.org/file/Special-Report_COVID-19-and-Academic-Governance.pdf.

Amoore, Louise. *The Politics of Possibility: Risk and Security Beyond Probability*. Durham, NC: Duke University Press, 2013.

Amsler, Sarah, and Keri Facer. "Contesting Anticipatory Regimes in Education: Exploring Alternative Educational Orientations to the Future." *Futures* 94 (2017): 6–14. https://doi.org/10.1016/j.futures.2017.01.001.

Arcade Fire. "Wasted Hours." Track 11 on *The Suburbs*. CD. Mercury, 2008–2010.

Arensdorf, Jill, and Janett Naylor-Tincknell. "Beyond the Traditional Retention Data: A Qualitative Study of the Social Benefits of Living Learning Communities." *Learning Communities Research and Practice* 4, no. 1 (2016): 1–16. https://files.eric.ed.gov/fulltext/EJ1112861.pdf.

Astin, Alexander W. *Four Critical Years: Effects of College on Beliefs, Attitudes, and Knowledge*. San Francisco: Jossey-Bass, 1977.

Astin, Alexander W. "The Methodology of Research on College Impact, Part One." *Sociology of Education* 45, no. 3 (Summer 1970): 223–54. https://www.jstor.org/stable/2112065.

Astin, Alexander W. "The Methodology of Research on College Impact, Part Two." *Sociology of Education* 45, no. 4 (Autumn 1970): 437–50. https://www.jstor.org/stable/2111842.

Astin, Alexander. W. "Student Involvement: A Developmental Theory for Higher Education." *Journal of College Student Personnel* 25, no. 4 (1984): 297–307.

Babb, Jim. "Progress Report: VCCS Student Onboarding and Enrollment Redesign Process Moving Forward." *VCCS Blog* (blog). Virginia Community College System, October 12, 2021. https://www.vccs.edu/blog/progress-report-vccs-student-onboarding-and-enrollment-redesign-process-moving-forward/.

Barad, Karen. *Meeting the Universe Halfway: Quantum Physics and the Entanglement of Matter and Meaning*. Durham, NC: Duke University Press, 2007.

Barger, Theresa Sullivan. "College Orientation: Making an Impact." *University Business*, November 26, 2018. https://universitybusiness.com/college-orientation-making-an-impact/.

Bauman, Dan. "After a Year of Losses, Higher Ed's Work Force Is Growing Again." *Chronicle of Higher Education*, July 8, 2021. https://www.chronicle.com/article/after-a-year-of-losses-higher-eds-work-force-is-growing-again.

Bauman, Dan. "Just Rewards? Some Colleges Cut Back During the Pandemic, But Not When It Came to Their Presidents' Pay Packages." *Chronicle of Higher Education*, November 30, 2021. https://www.chronicle.com/article/just-rewards.

Bauman, Dan. "The Pandemic Has Pushed Hundreds of Thousands of Workers Out of Higher Education." *Chronicle of Higher Education*, October 6, 2020. https://www.chronicle.com/article/how-the-pandemic-has-shrunk-higher-educations-work-force.

Berlant, Lauren. *Cruel Optimism*. Durham, NC: Duke University Press, 2011.

Berlant, Lauren. "Intuitionists: History and the Affective Event." *American Literary History* 20, no. 4 (2008): 845–60. https://www.muse.jhu.edu/article/254749.

Berlant, Lauren, and Kathleen Stewart. *The Hundreds*. Durham, NC: Duke University Press, 2019.

BETTY. "The L Word Theme." Recorded ca. 2004. Track 15 on *The L Word: The Second Season, Music From the Showtime Original Series*. Tommy Boy, Spotify.

Boggs, Doyle. "Making an Impact." *Wofford Today* (Summer 2014). https://www.wofford.edu/about/news/wofford-today/archive/2014/summer/making-an-impact.

Bowden, Jana Lay-Hwa, Leonie Tickle, and Kay Naumann. "The Four Pillars of Tertiary Student Engagement and Success: A Holistic Measurement

Approach." *Studies in Higher Education* 46, no. 6 (2019): 1207–24. https://doi.org/10.1080/03075079.2019.1672647.

Braidotti, Rosi. *Nomadic Subjects: Embodiment and Sexual Difference in Contemporary Feminist Theory.* 2nd ed. New York: Columbia University Press, 2011.

Braidotti, Rosi. *Nomadic Theory: The Portable Rosi Braidotti.* New York: Columbia University Press, 2011.

Braidotti, Rosi. *The Posthuman.* Cambridge, UK: Polity Press, 2013.

Brown, Wendy. *Undoing the Demos: Neoliberalism's Stealth Revolution.* Brooklyn, NY: Zone Books, 2015.

Burbules, Nicholas C., and C. K. Gunsalus. "Dealing With the Now." *Inside Higher Ed*, August 14, 2020. https://www.insidehighered.com/advice/2020/08/14/what-happens-next-weeks-will-turn-how-academic-leaders-make-choices-and-change-no.

Burke, Lilah. "Campus Zero." *Inside Higher Ed*, March 3, 2021. https://www.insidehighered.com/news/2021/03/03/first-college-impacted-covid-19-one-year-out.

Carlson, Scott, Eric Hoover, Beth McMurtrie, Emma Pettit, and Megan Zahneis. "Forced Out: The Faces of Higher Education's Historic Layoffs." *Chronicle of Higher Education*, March 19, 2021. https://www.chronicle.com/article/forced-out.

Chickering, Arthur W., and Zelda F. Gamson. "Seven Principles for Good Practice in Undergraduate Education." *AAHE Bulletin* 39, no. 7 (March 1987): 3–7. https://files.eric.ed.gov/fulltext/ED282491.pdf.

Chronicle Staff. "The Long Tail of an Unprecedented Crisis." *Chronicle of Higher Education*, November 18, 2020. https://www.chronicle.com/article/the-long-tail-of-an-unprecedented-crisis.

Coburn, Cynthia E. "Rethinking Scale: Moving Beyond Numbers to Deep and Lasting Change." *Educational Researcher* 32, no. 6 (August/September 2003): 3–12. https://doi.org/10.3102/0013189X032006003.

Cohen, Andy, exec. prod. *Real Housewives of Atlanta.* Season 6, episode 25, "Reunion Part 3." Featuring Nene Leakes. Aired May 4, 2014, on Bravo, Hulu.

College of Human Sciences & Education. *IMPACT: Improving Quality of Life Across the Lifespan.* Baton Rouge: Louisiana State University, 2018. https://issuu.com/lsuchse/docs/chse_impact_2017_final_issu_version.

The College of St. Scholastica. "Making an Impact." *The College of St. Scholastica News*, September 11, 2018. https://www.css.edu/about/news/making-an-impact/.

Commission on the Future of Higher Education. *A Test of Leadership: Charting the Future of U.S. Higher Education.* Washington, DC: US Department of Education, September 2006. https://files.eric.ed.gov/fulltext/ED493504.pdf.

Complete College America. *No Room for Doubt: Moving Corequisite Support from Idea to Imperative.* Indianapolis, IN: Complete College America, 2021. https://completecollege.org/wp-content/uploads/2021/04/CCA_NoRoomForDoubt_CorequisiteSupport.pdf.

Cukier, Kenneth, and Viktor Mayer-Schönberger. "The Dictatorship of Data." *MIT Technology Review*, May 31, 2013. https://www.technologyreview.com/2013/05/31/178263/the-dictatorship-of-data/.

Culp, Marguerite McGann, and Gwendolyn Jordan Dungy. *Building a Culture of Evidence in Student Affairs: A Guide for Leaders and Practitioners.* Washington, DC: NASPA-Student Affairs Administrators in Higher Education, 2012.

Darden College of Education and Professional Studies. *Making an Impact*: Darden College of Education and Professional Studies 2017–2018 Impact Report. Norfolk, VA: Old Dominion University, 2018. https://issuu.com/odueps/docs/report_7.

Daza, Stephanie, and Walter S. Gershon. "Beyond Ocular Inquiry: Sound, Silence, and Sonification." *Qualitative Inquiry* 21, no. 7 (2015): 639–44. https://doi.org/10.1177/1077800414566692.

de Certeau, Michel. *The Practice of Everyday Life.* Translated by Steven Randall. Berkeley: University of California Press, 1988.

de Freitas, Elizabeth. "Calculating Matter and Recombinant Subjects: The Infinitesimal and the Fractal Fold." *Cultural Studies ↔ Critical Methodologies* 16, no. 5 (2016): 462–70. https://doi.org/10.1177/1532708616655764.

de Freitas, Elizabeth, and Matthew X. Curinga. "New Materialist Approaches to the Study of Language and Identity: Assembling the Posthuman Subject." *Curriculum Inquiry* 45, no. 3 (2015): 249–65. http://dx.doi.org/10.1080/03626784.2015.1031059.

de Freitas, Elizabeth, and Francesca Ferrara. "Movement, Memory, and Mathematics: Henri Bergson and the Ontology of Learning." *Studies in Philosophy and Education* 34 (2015): 565–85. https://doi.org/10.1007/s11217-014-9455-y.

Deleuze, Gilles. *Difference and Repetition.* Translated by Paul Patton. New York: Columbia University Press, 1994.

Deleuze, Gilles. *The Logic of Sense.* Translated by Mark Lester and Charles Stivale. New York: Columbia University Press, 1990.

Deleuze, Gilles. "Postscript on the Societies of Control." *October* 59 (Winter 1992): 3–7. https://www.jstor.org/stable/778828.

Deleuze, Gilles, and Felix Guattari. *A Thousand Plateaus: Capitalism and Schizophrenia.* Translated by Brian Massumi. Minneapolis: University of Minnesota Press, 1987.

Denna, Eric. "The Business Model of Higher Education." *Viewpoints* (blog), *EDUCAUSE Review*, March 24, 2014. https://er.educause.edu/articles/2014/3/the-business-model-of-higher-education.

Diep, Francie. "A Covid 'New Normal' Is Coming to Campus. Here's What That Could Look Like." *Chronicle of Higher Education*, January 14, 2022. https://www.chronicle.com/article/a-covid-new-normal-is-coming-to-campus-heres-what-that-could-look-like.

Doherty, Heather. "100 Years of Making an Impact: OSU's Counseling Program Celebrates Milestone Anniversary." *Campus News, Oregon State University*, December 8, 2017. https://ecampus.oregonstate.edu/news/2017/100-years-of-counselor-education/.

Engstrom, Cathy McHugh, and Vincent Tinto. "Learning Better Together: The Impact of Learning Communities on the Persistence of Low-Income Students." *Opportunity Matters: A Journal of Research Informing Educational Opportunity Practice and Programs* 1 (2008): 5–21. http://www.pellinstitute.org/downloads/opportunity_matters-JAOE_Volume_01_2008.pdf#page=7.

Esters, Lorenzo. "Making an Impact in Higher Education Equity." *Strata Education Network*, February 8, 2018. https://stradaeducation.org/navigating-education/making-an-impact-in-higher-education-equity/.

Ewell, Peter T. "To Capture the Ineffable: New Forms of Assessment in Higher Education." *Review of Research in Education* 17, no. 1 (1991): 75–125. https://doi.org/10.3102/0091732X017001075.

Farnham, Nicholas H., and Adam Yarmolinsky, eds. *Rethinking Liberal Education*. New York: Oxford University Press, 1996.

Feldman, Kenneth A., and Theodore Mead Newcomb. *The Impact of College on Students, Volume 1: An Analysis of Four Decades of Research*. San Francisco: Jossey-Bass, 1969.

Fineman, Joel. "The History of the Anecdote: Fiction and Fiction." In *The New Historicism*, edited by H. Aram Veeser, 49–76. London: Routledge, 2013.

Foucault, Michel. *The History of Sexuality Volume 1: The Will to Know*. Translated by Robert Hurley. New York: Vintage, 1990.

Foucault, Michel. *The Order of Things: An Archaeology of the Human Sciences*. New York: Vintage, 1994.

Freeman, Melissa. *Modes of Thinking in Qualitative Data Analysis*. New York: Routledge, 2016.

Friga, Paul N. "Under Covid-19, University Budgets Like We've Never Seen Before." *Chronicle of Higher Education*, April 20, 2020. https://www.chronicle.com/article/under-covid-19-university-budgets-like-weve-never-seen-before/.

Gagliardi, Jonathan S., Amelia Parnell, and Julia Carpenter-Hubin, eds. *The Analytics Revolution in Higher Education: Big Data, Organizational Learning, and Student Success*. Sterling, VA: Stylus, 2018.

Gardner, Lee. "The Great Contraction." *Chronicle of Higher Education*, February 15, 2021. https://www.chronicle.com/article/the-great-contraction.

Gershon, Walter S. "Vibrational Affect: Sound Theory and Practice in Qualitative Research." *Cultural Studies ↔ Critical Methodologies* 13, no. 4 (2013): 257–62. https://doi.org/10.1177/1532708613488067.

Gregg, Melissa. *Counterproductive: Time Management in the Knowledge Economy*. Durham, NC: Duke University Press, 2018.

Gregg, Melissa, and Gregory J. Siegworth, eds. *The Affect Theory Reader.* Durham, NC: Duke University Press, 2010.

Groves, Christopher. "Emptying the Future: On the Environmental Politics of Anticipation." *Futures* 92 (2016): 29–38. http://dx.doi.org/10.1016/j.futures.2016.06.003.

Gullion, Jessica Smartt. *Diffractive Ethnography: Social Sciences and the Ontological Turn.* New York: Routledge, 2018.

Hacking, Ian. "Making Up People." In *Reconstructing Individualism*, edited by Thomas C. Miller, Morton Sosna, and David E. Wellbery, 222–36. Stanford, CA: Stanford University Press, 1986.

Harney, Stefano, and Fred Moten. *The Undercommons: Fugitive Planning and Black Study.* Wivenhoe, UK: Minor Compositions, 2013. https://www.minorcompositions.info/wp-content/uploads/2013/04/undercommons-web.pdf.

Hatch, Deryl K. "Unpacking the Black Box of Student Engagement: The Need for Programmatic Investigation of High Impact Practices." *Community College Journal of Research and Practice* 36, no. 11 (2012): 903–15. https://doi.org/10.1080/10668926.2012.690319.

Hatch, Deryl K., and E. Michael Bohlig. "An Empirical Typology of the Latent Programmatic Structure of Community College Student Success Programs." *Research in Higher Education* 57 (2016): 72–98. https://doi.org/10.1007/s11162-015-9379-6/.

Hill, Patrick. "The Rationale for Learning Communities." Speech given at the Inaugural Conference on Learning Communities, Washington Center for Undergraduate Education, Olympia, WA, October 22, 1985. http://www.evergreen.edu/sites/default/files/facultydevelopment/docs/patrickhillrationale.pdf.

Holt, Emily A., and Amanda Nielson. "Learning Communities and Unlinked Sections: A Contrast of Student Backgrounds, Student Outcomes, and In-Class Experiences." *Research in Higher Education* 60: 670–83. https://doi.org/10.1007/s11162-018-9531-1.

Holy See. *The Order for Funerals, For Use by the Ordinariates Erected Under the Auspices of the Apostolic Constitution* Anglicanorum cœtibus. Houston, TX: Ordinariate of the Chair of Saint Peter, 2012. https://ordinariate.net/documents/resources/AC_Order_for_Funerals.pdf.

Hoover, Eric. "Here's Why More Colleges Are Extending Deposit Deadlines—and Why Some Aren't. *Chronicle of Higher Education*, March 18, 2020. https://www.chronicle.com/article/heres-why-more-colleges-are-extending-deposit-deadlines-and-why-some-arent/.

Hoover, Eric. "Our Relationship With Tests Is Unraveling. Why Is Everyone So Conflicted About It?" *Chronicle of Higher Education*, July 29, 2020. https://www.chronicle.com/article/crisis-is-changing-the-debate-over-standardized-exams-but-our-relationship-with-them-is-as-conflicted-as-ever.

Huba, Mary E., Shari Ellertson, Michelle D. Cook, and Douglas L. Epperson. "Assessment's Role in Transforming a Grass Roots Initiative into an Institutionalized Program: Evaluating and Shaping Learning Communities at Iowa State University." In *Doing Learning Community Assessment: Five Campus Stories*, edited by Jean MacGregor, 20–47. Olympia: National Learning Communities Project, 2003. http://wacenter.evergreen.edu/node/1744.

Hubler, Shawn. "Colleges Slash Budgets in the Pandemic, With 'Nothing Off Limits.'" *New York Times*, November 2, 2020. https://www.nytimes.com/2020/10/26/us/colleges-coronavirus-budget-cuts.html.

Jackson, Alecia Y., and Lisa A. Mazzei. *Thinking With Theory in Qualitative Research: Viewing Data Across Multiple Perspectives*. London: Routledge, 2012.

Jaffee, David. "Peer Cohorts and the Unintended Consequences of Freshman Learning Communities." *College Teaching* 55, no. 2 (Spring 2007): 65–71. https://www.jstor.org/stable/27559314.

Jarke, Juliane, and Andreas Breiter. "Editorial: The Datafication of Education." *Learning, Media and Technology* 44, no. 1 (2019): 1–6. https://doi.org/10.1080/17439884.2019.1573833.

Jones, Emma. "How The Wire Became the Greatest TV Show Ever Made." *BBC*, April 13, 2018. https://www.bbc.com/culture/article/20180412-how-the-wire-became-the-greatest-tv-show-ever-made.

Kahu, Ella R. "Framing Student Engagement in Higher Education." *Studies in Higher Education* 38, no. 5 (2013): 758–73. http://dx.doi.org/10.1080/03075079.2011.598505.

Keeling, Kara. *Queer Times, Black Futures*. New York: New York University Press, 2019.

Kelchen, Robert. "Permanent Budget Cuts Are Coming." *Chronicle of Higher Education*, October 15, 2020. https://www.chronicle.com/article/permanent-budget-cuts-are-coming.

Kezar, Adrianna, Tom DePaola, and Daniel T. Scott. *The Gig Academy: Mapping Labor in the Neoliberal Academy*. Baltimore: Johns Hopkins University Press, 2019.

Koopman, Colin. *Genealogy as Critique: Foucault and the Problems of Modernity*. Bloomington: Indiana University Press, 2013.

Kuh, George D. *High-Impact Educational Practices: What They Are, Who Has Access to Them, and Why They Matter*. Washington, DC: Association of American Colleges and Universities, 2008.

Kuh, George D. "What Student Affairs Professionals Need to Know About Student Engagement." *Journal of College Student Development* 50, no. 6 (November/December 2009): 683–706. https://doi.org/10.1353/csd.0.0099.

Kuh, George D. "What We're Learning About Student Engagement From NSSE: Benchmarks for Effective Educational Practices." *Change* 35, no. 2 (2003): 24–32. https://www.jstor.org/stable/40177261.

Kuh, George D., Jillian Kinzie, Jennifer A. Buckley, Brian K. Bridges, and John C. Hayek. "Piecing Together the Student Success Puzzle: Research, Propositions, and Recommendations." *ASHE Higher Education Report* 32, no. 5 (2007). https://doi.org/10.1002/aehe.3205.

Kuh, George D., Jillian Kinzie, Jennifer A. Buckley, Brian K. Bridges, and John C. Hayek. *What Matters to Student Success: A Review of the Literature.* Washington, DC: National Postsecondary Education Cooperative, July 2006. https://nces.ed.gov/npec/pdf/Kuh_Team_Report.pdf.

Kuh, George D., Jillian Kinzie, Ty Cruce, Rick Shoup, and Robert M. Gonyea. *Connecting the Dots: Multi-Faceted Analyses of the Relationships between Student Engagement Results from the NSSE, and the Institutional Practices and Conditions That Foster Student Success.* Bloomington, IN: Center for Postsecondary Research, January 2, 2007. https://scholarworks.iu.edu/dspace/handle/2022/23684.

Kuh, George D., Jillian Kinzie, John H. Schuh, Elizabeth J. Whitt, and associates. *Student Success in College: Creating Conditions That Matter.* San Francisco: Jossey-Bass, 2010.

Kuh, George D., and Ken O'Donnell. *Ensuring Quality and Taking High-Impact Practices to Scale.* Washington, DC: Association of American Colleges and Universities, 2013.

Kuntz, Aaron M. *The Responsible Methodologist: Inquiry, Truth-Telling, and Social Justice.* London: Routledge, 2015.

la paperson. *A Third University is Possible.* Minneapolis: University of Minnesota Press, 2017.

Lederman, Doug. "Will Shift to Remote Teaching Be Boon or Bane for Online Learning?" *Inside Higher Ed*, March 18, 2020. https://www.insidehighered.com/digital-learning/article/2020/03/18/most-teaching-going-remote-will-help-or-hurt-online-learning.

Lenning, Oscar T., and Larry H. Ebbers. "The Powerful Potential of Learning Communities: Improving Education for the Future." *ASHE-ERIC Higher Education Report* 26, no. 6 (1999). https://files.eric.ed.gov/fulltext/ED428606.pdf.

Lorenz, Chris. "If You're So Smart, Why Are You Under Surveillance? Universities, Neoliberalism, and New Public Management." *Critical Inquiry* 38, no. 3 (Spring 2012): 599–629. https://doi.org/10.1086/664553.

Love, Anne Goodsell. "The Growth and Current State of Learning Communities in Higher Education." *New Directions for Teaching and Learning* no. 132 (Winter 2012): 5–18. https://doi.org/10.1002/tl.20032.

Macfarlane, Bruce, and Michael Tomlinson. "Critical and Alternative Perspectives on Student Engagement." *Higher Education Policy* 30, no. 1 (2017): 1–4. https://doi.org/10.1057/s41307-016-0026-4.

Macgilchrist, Felicitas, John Potter, and Ben Williamson. "Shifting Scales of Research on Learning, Media and Technology." *Learning, Media and Technology* 46, no. 4 (2021): 369–76. https://doi.org/10.1080/17439884.2021.1994418.

MacLure, Maggie. "Researching Without Representation? Language and Materiality in Post-Qualitative Methodology." *International Journal of Qualitative Studies in Education* 26, no. 6 (2013): 658–67. https://doi.org/10.1080/095 18398.2013.788755.

Manning, Erin. *The Minor Gesture.* Durham, NC: Duke University Press, 2016.

Manning, Erin. "For a Pragmatics of the Useless, or the Value of the Infrathin." *Political Theory* 45, no. 1 (2017): 97–115. https://doi.org/10.1177/0090591715625877.

Manning, Erin. "Propositions For a Radical Pedagogy, or How to Rethink Value." In *Affect in Literacy Learning and Teaching: Pedagogies, Politics, and Coming to Know,* edited by Kevin M. Leander and Christian Ehret, 43–49. New York: Routledge, 2019.

Massumi, Brian. *99 Theses on the Revaluation of Value: A Postcapitalist Manifesto.* Minneapolis: University of Minnesota Press, 2018.

Massumi, Brian. *Ontopower: War, Powers, and the State of Perception.* Durham, NC: Duke University Press, 2015.

Massumi, Brian. *Parables for the Virtual: Movement, Affect, Sensation.* Durham, NC: Duke University Press, 2002.

Mayhew, Matthew J., Alyssa N. Rockenbach, Nicholas A. Bowman, Tricia A. D. Seifert, and Gregory C. Wolniak. *How College Affects Students, Volume 3: 21st Century Evidence that Higher Education Works.* San Francisco: Jossey-Bass, 2016.

McConnell, Kate Drezek, and Terrel Rhodes. *On Solid Ground: VALUE Report 2017.* Washington, DC: American Association of Colleges and Universities. https://www.aacu.org/publication/on-solid-ground-value-report-2017.

McKay, Adam, dir. *The Big Short.* 2015; Beverly Hills, CA: Plan B Entertainment, 2015. Netflix.

McMahon, Walter W. *Higher Learning, Greater Good: The Private and Social Benefits of Higher Education.* Baltimore: Johns Hopkins University Press, 2017.

Meiklejohn, Alexander. "Wisconsin's Experimental College." *The Journal of Higher Education,* 1, no. 9 (1930): 485–90. https://doi.org/10.2307/1974761.

Miller, Graham N. S., and Christopher C. Morphew. "Merchants of Optimism: Agenda-Setting Organizations and the Framing of Performance-Based Funding for Higher Education." *The Journal of Higher Education* 88, no. 5 (2017): 754–84. https://doi.org/10.1080/00221546.2017.1313084.

Mintz, Steven. "Let's Not Return to the Old Normal." *Inside Higher Ed,* February 23, 2021. https://www.insidehighered.com/blogs/higher-ed-gamma/let's-not-return-old-normal.

Mol, Annemarie. *The Body Multiple: Ontology in Medical Practice.* Durham, NC: Duke University Press, 2003.

Morris, Libby V. "Mining Data for Student Success." *Innovative Higher Education* 41, no. 3 (2016): 183–85. https://doi.org/10.1007/s10755-016-9367-6.

Mowrer, O. H., and A. D. Ullman. "Time as a Determinant in Integrative Learning." *Psychological Review* 52, no. 2 (1945): 61–90. https://doi.org/10.1037/h0057071.

Mulcahy, Daniel G. *The Educated Person: Toward a New Paradigm for Liberal Education.* Lanham, MD: Rowman & Littlefield. 2008.

Musoba, Glenda D., Veronica A. Jones, and Tekla Nicholas. "From Open Door to Limited Access: Transfer Students and the Challenges of Choosing a Major." *Journal of College Student Development* 59, no. 6 (2018): 716–33. https://doi.org/10.1353/csd.2018.0067.

National Survey of Student Engagement. *Engagement Insights: Survey Findings on the Quality of Undergraduate Education: Annual Results 2019.* Bloomington, IN: Center for Postsecondary Research, 2020. https://scholarworks.iu.edu/dspace/bitstream/handle/2022/25321/NSSE_2019_Annual_Results.pdf?sequence=1&isAllowed=y.

National Survey of Student Engagement. *Experiences That Matter: Enhancing Student Learning and Student Success: Annual Report 2007.* Bloomington, IN: Center for Postsecondary Research, 2007. https://scholarworks.iu.edu/dspace/bitstream/handle/2022/23412/NSSE_2007_Annual_Report.pdf?sequence=1&isAllowed=y.

Newfield, Christopher. *The Great Mistake: How We Wrecked Public Universities and How We Can Fix Them.* Baltimore: Johns Hopkins University Press, 2016.

Newman, John Henry. *The Idea of a University: Defined and Illustrated.* London: Basil Montagu Pickering, 1873.

Nike. "Next Long Run." *Nike Run Club.* V. 7.30. Nike, 2023.

Paige, Susan Mary, Amitra A. Wall, Joseph J. Marren, Amy DiBartolo Rockwell, and Brian Dubenion. *The Learning Community Experience in Higher Education: High-Impact Practice for Student Retention.* New York: Routledge, 2017.

Panos, Robert J., and Alexander W. Astin. "Attrition Among College Students." *American Educational Research Journal* 5, no. 1 (January 1968): 57–72. https://doi.org/10.3102/00028312005001057.

Pascarella, Ernest T., and Patrick T. Terenzini. *How College Affects Students: Findings and Insights from Twenty Years of Research.* San Francisco: Jossey-Bass, 1991.

Pascarella, Ernest T., and Patrick T. Terenzini. *How College Affects Students, Volume 2: A Third Decade of Research.* San Francisco: Jossey-Bass, 2005.

Payne, Emily. "Making an Impact: MCS Graduate's 'Nooks' Upgrade Campus Spaces for Students." *Mellon College of Science News & Events*, December 15, 2020. https://www.cmu.edu/mcs/news-events/2020/1215_cory-bird.html.

Perna, Laura W. "Throwing Down the Gauntlet: Ten Ways to Ensure That Higher Education Research Continues to Matter." *The Review of Higher Education* 39, no. 3 (2016): 319–38. https://doi.org/10.1353/rhe.2016.0016.

Pettit, Emma. "Covid-19 Cuts Hit Contingent Faculty Hard. As the Pandemic Drags On, Some Question Their Future." *Chronicle of Higher Education*, October 26, 2020. https://www.chronicle.com/article/covid-19-cuts-hit-contingent-faculty-hard-as-it-drags-on-some-question-their-future.

Pike, Gary R., George D. Kuh, and Alexander C. McCormick. "An Investigation of the Contingent Relationships Between Learning Community Participation and Student Engagement." *Research in Higher Education* 52 (2011): 300–322. https://doi.org/10.1007/s11162-010-9192-1.

Postsecondary Value Commission. *Equitable Value: Promoting Economic Mobility and Social Justice through Postsecondary Education.* May, 2021. https://post secondaryvalue.org/wp-content/uploads/2021/05/PVC-Final-Report-FINAL. pdf.

Potter, Claire Bond. "The Only Way to Save Higher Education Is to Make It Free." *New York Times*, June 5, 2020. https://www.nytimes.com/2020/06/05/opinion/ sunday/free-college-tuition-coronavirus.html.

Radiohead. "Fitter Happier." Track 7 on *OK Computer*. CD. Los Angeles: Capitol Records, 1996–1997.

Raunig, Gerald. *Dividuum: Machinic Capitalism and Molecular Revolution.* Translated by Aileen Derieg. South Pasadena, CA: Semiotext(e), 2016.

Regele, Matthew D. "Pedagogy and Profit? Efforts to Develop and Sell Digital Courseware Products for Higher Education." *American Educational Research Journal* 57, no. 3 (June 2020): 1125–58. https://doi.org/10.3102/0002831219869234.

Ribera, Amy K., Angie L. Miller, and Amber D. Dumford. "Sense of Peer Belonging and Institutional Acceptance in the First Year: The Role of High-Impact Practices." *Journal of College Student Development* 58, no. 4 (May 2017): 543–63. https://doi.org/10.1353/csd.2017.0042.

Robinson, Bradley, and Mel Kutner. "Spinoza and the Affective Turn: A Return to the Philosophical Origins of Affect." *Qualitative Inquiry* 25, no. 2 (2019): 111–17. https://doi.org/10.1177/1077800418786312.

Roth, Michael. "Pragmatic Liberal Education." *New Literary History* 44, no. 4 (2013): 521–38. https://doi.org/10.1353/nlh.2013.0036.

Saraiya, Sonia. "15 Years Later, 2017 Needs Its Own 'The Wire.'" *Variety*, June 1, 2017. https://variety.com/2017/tv/news/the-wire-anniversary-15-years-1202450469/.

Schapiro, Morton O. "Let's Not Return to Normal When the 'New Normal' Finally Arrives." *Chronicle of Higher Education*, July 29, 2021. https://www.chronicle. com/article/lets-not-return-to-normal-when-the-new-normal-finally-arrives.

Sharpe, Christina. *In the Wake: On Blackness and Being.* Durham, NC: Duke University Press, 2016.

Sharpe, Christina. *Ordinary Notes.* New York: Farrar, Straus and Giroux, 2023.

Sheffield, Rob. "100 Greatest TV Shows of All Time." *Rolling Stone*, September 21, 2016. https://www.rollingstone.com/tv/tv-lists/100-greatest-tv-shows-of-all-time-105998/.

Siegworth, Gregory J., and Melissa Gregg. "An Inventory of Shimmers." In *The Affect Theory Reader*, edited by Melissa Gregg and Gregory J. Siegworth, 1–25. Durham, NC: Duke University Press, 2010.

Simon, David. *The Wire.* Blown Deadline Productions, HBO Max, 2002–2008.

Smith, Barbara Leigh. "The Challenge of Learning Communities as a Growing National Movement." *Peer Review* 4, no. 1 (Summer/Fall 2001): 4–8. https://eric.ed.gov/?id=EJ647377.

Smith, Barbara Leigh, Jean MacGregor, Roberta S. Matthews, and Faith Gabelnick. *Learning Communities: Reforming Undergraduate Education.* San Francisco, CA: Jossey-Bass, 2004.

Smith, Rachel A. "Magnets and Seekers: A Network Perspective on Academic Integration Inside Two Residential Communities." *The Journal of Higher Education* 86, no. 6 (November/December 2015): 893–922. https://doi.org/10.1353/jhe.2015.0033.

Smithers, Laura Elizabeth. "How Should Institutions of Higher Education Define and Measure Student Success? Student Success as Liberal Education Escapes Definition and Measurement." In *Contested Issues in Troubled Times: Student Affairs Dialogues About Equity, Civility, and Safety,* edited by Peter Magolda, Marcia Baxter-Magolda, and Rozana Carducci, 127–37. Sterling, VA: Stylus, 2019.

Smithers, Laura. "Reconceptualizing College Impact Studies Through a Fractal Assemblage Theory." *Philosophy and Theory in Higher Education* 2, no. 2 (2020): 89–114. https://doi.org/10.3726/PTIHE022020.0005.

Smithers, Laura. "Student Success as Preemption: Predictive Constructions of Futures-to-Never-Come." *Futures* 124 (December 2020): 1–10. https://doi.org/10.1016/j.futures.2020.102639.

Snaza, Nathan. "Ethologies of Education." *Cultural Studies ↔ Critical Methodologies* 20, no. 3 (2020): 261–71. https://doi.org/10.1177/1532708619873881.

Soldner, Laura, Yvonne Lee, and Paul Duby. "Welcome to the Block: Developing Freshman Learning Communities That Work." *Journal of College Student Retention* 1, no. 2 (1999): 115–29. https://doi.org/10.2190/QL13-7QWA-VDXF-PJHL.

Spinoza, Baruch. *Ethics.* In *Ethics; Treatise on the Emendation of the Intellect; Selected Letters.* 2nd ed. Edited by Seymour Feldman, 31–223. Indianapolis, IN: Hackett, 1992.

Springgay, Stephanie, and Sarah E. Truman. *Walking Methodologies in a More-Than-Human World: WalkingLab.* London: Routledge, 2018.

Stanwood, Les, and Lynn Dunlap. "The Assessment Chase: The Changing Shape of Assessment in Shaping Change at Skagit Valley College." In *Doing Learning Community Assessment: Five Campus Stories,* edited by Jean MacGregor, 74–96. Olympia, WA: National Learning Communities Project, 2003. http://wacenter.evergreen.edu/node/1744.

Stewart, Kathleen. *Ordinary Affects.* Durham, NC: Duke University Press, 2007.

St. Pierre, Elizabeth A. "The Empirical and the New Empiricisms." *Cultural Studies ↔ Critical Methodologies* 16, no. 2 (2016): 111–24. https://doi.org/10.1177/1532708616636147.

St. Pierre, Elizabeth Adams. "Writing Post Qualitative Inquiry." *Qualitative Inquiry* 24, no. 9 (2018): 603–8. https://doi.org/10.1177/1077800417734567.

Study Group on the Conditions of Excellence in American Higher Education. *Involvement in learning: Realizing the potential of American Higher Education.* Washington, DC: Department of Education, October 1984. http://files.eric.ed.gov/fulltext/ED246833.pdf.

Tatum, Beverly Daniel. *Why Are All the Black Kids Sitting Together in the Cafeteria: And Other Conversations About Race.* New York: Basic Books, 1997.

Tinto, Vincent. "Dropout from Higher Education: A Theoretical Synthesis of Recent Research." *Review of Educational Research* 45, no. 1 (Winter 1975): 89–125. https://doi.org/10.3102/00346543045001089.

Tinto, Vincent. "Learning Better Together: The Impact of Learning Communities on Student Success." *Higher Education Monograph Series* 1 (2003): 1–8. https://home.ubalt.edu/ub78l45/My%20Library/storage/5NFTFFWB/Learning20Better20Together.pdf.

Tinto, Vincent. "What Have We Learned About the Impact of Learning Communities on Students?" *Assessment UPdate* 12, no. 2 (March–April 2000): 1–2, 12.

Tukibayeva, Malika, and Robert M. Gonyea. (2014). "High-Impact Practices and the First-Year Student." *New Directions for Institutional Research* 2013, no. 160 (2014): 19–35. http://doi.wiley.com/10.1002/ir.20059.

University of Colorado. *Making an Impact.* Accessed December 11, 2023. https://www.cu.edu/pridepoints.

van Dijck, José. "Datafication, Dataism and Dataveillance: Big Data Between Scientific Paradigm and Ideology." *Surveillance and Society* 12, no. 2 (2014): 197–208. https://doi.org/10.24908/ss.v12i2.4776.

Virginia Peninsula Community College. "Making an Impact for More Than 40 Years." *Virginia Peninsula Community College News*, July 21, 2021. https://www.vpcc.edu/news/2021/07/making-impact-more-40-years.html.

Watermark Insights. "Integrating Artificial and Human Intelligence for Student Success." *Watermark* (blog). May 25, 2023. https://www.watermarkinsights.com/resources/blog/integrating-artificial-and-human-intelligence-for-student-success.

Watermark Insights. "The Outcomes of Success Coaching." *Watermark* (blog), April 20, 2023. https://www.watermarkinsights.com/resources/blog/the-outcomes-of-success-coaching.

Wells, Ryan S., Ethan A. Kolek, Elizabeth A. Williams, and Daniel B. Saunders. (2015). "'How We Know What We Know:' A Systematic Comparison of Research Methods Employed in Higher Education Journals, 1996–2000 v. 2006–2010." *Journal of Higher Education* 86, no. 2 (2015): 171–95. https://doi.org/10.1080/00221546.2015.11777361.

Whitford, Emma. "Fall Brings Wave of Furloughs." *Inside Higher Ed*, September 2, 2020. https://www.insidehighered.com/news/2020/09/02/colleges-furlough-more-employees.

Wolf-Wendel, Lisa, Kelly Ward, and Jillian Kinzie. (2009). "A Tangled Web of Terms: The Overlap and Unique Contribution of Involvement, Engagement, and Integration to Understanding College Student Success." *Journal of College Student Development* 50, no. 4 (July/August 2009): 407–28. https://doi.org/10.1353/csd.0.0077.

Wolgemuth, Jennifer R., Travis M. Marn, Tim Barko, and Marcus Weaver-Hightower. "Radical Uncertainty Is Not Enough: (In)Justice Matters of Post-Qualitative Research." *International Review of Qualitative Research* 14, no. 2 (2022): 575–93. https://doi.org/10.1177/19408447211012658.

Zakaria, Fareed. *In Defense of a Liberal Education.* New York: W. W. Norton, 2015.

Zepke, Nick. "Student Engagement in Neo-Liberal Times: What Is Missing?" *Higher Education Research and Development* 37, no. 2 (2018): 433–46. https://doi.org/10.1080/07294360.2017.1370440.

Zhao, Chun-Mei, and George D. Kuh. "Adding Value: Learning Communities and Student Engagement." *Research in Higher Education* 45 no. 2 (March 2004): 115–38. https://www.jstor.org/stable/40197341.

Zilvinskis, John, Anthony A. Masseria, and Gary R. Pike. "Student Engagement and Student Learning: Examining the Convergent and Discriminant Validity of the Revised National Survey of Student Engagement." *Research in Higher Education* 58 (2017): 880–8903. https://doi.org/10.1007/s11162-017-9450-6.

Index

master narratives, 153
McNamara, Robert, 136
mediation, 10, 33, 65, 147–48
methodology of this study, 11, 183n42
metricization, 1, 5, 41, 136, 174
Mexican people, 61
middle-class values, 30–31
monogamy, 31, 75
monopoly, 24–25
monotony, 102–3
movement, 6, 180, 183n41
music, 21–22, 62, 66, 72, 86–87, 127

names: of learning community, 67
narrative: causality as, 7; integrative
    learning as space apart from, 74;
    master narratives, 153; palpability
    and, 9
National Survey of Student
    Engagement (NSSE), 37, 57, 129
neoliberalism, 86, 109, 190n17
nervousness, shimmers of, 18
new normals, ix–x, 3, 82, 98, 149,
    172, 179
noise, 28, 61, 66, 74
normalization, 104, 159
notes: color-coding, 162; students
    actively taking, 35, 94, 99, 131,
    159, 162, 167; students not actively
    taking, 72, 129, 133–34; students'
    perspective on, 55. See also field
    notes
noteworthiness, 70–71

observation as data collection, 120
office hours, 127, 159
ontogenesis, 141
optimization, 2, 5, 109, 119
order of things (digital), 79
ordinary: high-impact practices and,
    6, 176; intensities and possibilities
    of, 5–6; narrative and, 9; ordinary

affects, 7, 97; ordinary impact,
    36–37, 98, 176–77; as (not)
    outcome, 168–69; practices of, 97;
    representation and, 5–6; re/valuing
    the, 28, 108, 168, 174–75; vs. scale,
    6; structuring devices and, 176–77
orientation, 15, 27, 134, 143
origin stories, 27, 43–44
outcomes, 2, 57, 135, 168–69

palpability and narrative, 9
participant observation, 8
parties, 114
pedagogy (radical), 96
peer mentors: feedback from, 22–24,
    64; introductions from, 39, 151,
    172–73; leadership from, 16–17,
    93–94, 113–14, 121–22, 134–35,
    164–65, 169; on resident assistants,
    140; student questions to, 66–67;
    students on, 48–49; support for,
    23–24; talking to each other,
    127–28; talking to students, 72, 89,
    105–6, 120, 123–24, 141, 151, 161,
    163
peer-to-peer advising, 13, 14
pessimism, 65
philanthropy, 75
plastic consumption, 65
politics of location (collective and
    social), 9
postgraduation employment, 26, 28
pot (marijuana), 128–29
potentiality and affect, 97
PowerPoint presentations. See slide
    presentations
practice: abstractions of, 180; vs.
    theory, 141
presence (researcher), 6, 9, 164
prestige, 62
priorities, competition between, 31–32
prison, 20–21